MW01283184

THE SCIENCE OF DEPARTURES

THE SCIENCE OF DEPARTURES

Adalber Salas Hernández

Translated by Robin Myers

KENNING EDITIONS: 2021

Published in 2021 by Kenning Editions.

ISBN: 978-1-7343176-6-4
Library of Congress Control Number: 2021941969

Distributed by Small Press Distribution
1341 Seventh St., Berkeley, CA 94710
Spdbooks.org

Cover design by Faride Mereb.
Cover title font: Tethys by Mirko Velimirović.
Cover art: *Still Life with Fern and Insects* (2018) by Eileen Hohmuth-Lemonick.
Interior composition by Patrick Durgin.
Set in Miller and Akzidenz-Grotesk.

This book was made possible in part by the supporters of Kenning Editions: Alan Bernheimer, Jay Besemer, Mark Booth, Joel Craig, Ian Dreiblatt, Joseph Giardini, Katherine M. Hedeen, Krystal Languell, Joslyn Layne, Olivia Lott, Pamela Lu, Olivia DiNapoli, Thomas Troolin, and The John A. Hartford Foundation.

The publisher gratefully acknowledges the support of Softandnet Inc. in the making of this edition.

The first edition of *La ciencia de las despedidas* was published by Editorial Pre-Textos (2018).

Several of the translations in this book were first published in the following journals: VI, VII, and XVII in *Circumference*; XXVIII, XI, and XXII in *Harvard Review*; XVIII, XIX, XXIII, and XXIV in *Kenyon Review*; I in *Plume*, and; XIII and XXXIII in *Waxwing*.

Kenning Editions is a 501c3 non-profit, independent literary publisher investigating the relationships of aesthetic quality to political commitment. Consider donating or subscribing: Kenningeditions.com/shop/donation

For Malena Salas Robertson

In memory of Obdulia Castañeda

THE SCIENCE OF DEPARTURES

E come a li orbi non approda il Sole,
Così a l'ombre, quivi ond'io parlo ora,
Luce del ciel di sè largir non vuole.

Dante Alighieri, *Purgatorio*

I
(ONE-WAY TICKET)

We study the departure screen and the
next flight
and the next
and the next,
each taking off with the same
deaf precision, like obedient children,
fearing the divine and punishing hand. The sky won't
embrace them as devoutly as they think;
all it offers is insomnia, turbulence,
and sedatives to navigate the clouds
without panicking.

Lines of people, luggage, handbags,
receipts, memories strewn like sawdust
across the floor. All
impatient, with a nervous hunger
that empties things out from the inside, gifting them
the hard paradise of waiting
and escape.

Airports, hospitals, the same harsh
spotlessness, the same grayed light, as if
all that white could eclipse
the bodies as they come and
go, cancel out the excreted fluids,
the tender sweat
that's ultimately the only evidence
of our passing through this place.
There's not a single organ made
for vanishing like this. Just the body trimmed,
uncomfortably neat, barely recognizing

itself in the flight number, the gate
number, the skinny air
we choke on in the pre-op.
                                        (But meanwhile,
who designs these entry forms, who selects
the ticket font and size, who
instills them with their taste for getting lost?)
                                                                        The body,
knot of valves, fatty matter, taut with ligaments.
The body stupefied by the engines' lilt,
the noise of hungry time
scratching seams into our flesh.
That's the sound of hunger: like the next flight.

Then I look at your hands, which are always
damp and blunt
the cutting edge of everything they touch.
I watch their skin, astonished and afraid,
as they grip your ticket, check
your pockets for
your papers,
holy cards with saints and votives on offer—

as the airport ceiling
lifts and starts to fly, baring us
beneath the sky of sand.

II

Odysseus never returned to Ithaca. He spent too many years
at sea, chewed up by those great sad jaws.
So many years that even the gods
tired of watching and chasing after him
and nodded off. When
he came back, he didn't look the same. No signs
identified him; he had no marks
or scars. Nor was he carrying a passport or
ID card. He looked more like
a Turkish youth or a scrawny Cypriot with
a few gray hairs and sun-
browned skin. He made it to shore when his ship
went down. The island had no name that he
could understand: its craggy bluffs and forests
smelled different, and its birds sang in their sleep.
A stony lizard island in the midday heat.
He couldn't find his palace, no dark, hardworking Penelopes,
no short-bearded Telemachuses. There were no suitors
anywhere in sight; maybe someone had already killed them off.
All he found was a village with a couple streets,
exasperated by the light, the creaking of the tin-
colored waves. No one recognized him, nor he
anyone else. Dogs sounded as he passed,
their barks like the garbled shine of bronze.
Confused, he decided to sail onward to the continent.
But the old custom of hospitality
had been lost; no one was willing anymore
to trade a roof for a story or
a song. He was imprisoned for his lack
of documents and for speaking in an incomprehensible
tongue that snapped like ancient bones.
It was as if everyone had plugged

their ears with beeswax. He tried to explain
that traveling means language lost, not gained, but
it was all for naught. In jail, he was unable to
recount his tales to anyone, couldn't tell
the other prisoners of his feats: for the first time, he
was truly naked. His battle crimes
embedded deeper in his memory, like dates
leaking a quiet, brutal odor as they rot.
With the deftness he was famous for, he managed to escape
after a few months, this time blinding no one.
He settled in a lonely part
of town, near the sawmills. There he found
work as a carpenter, though who knows how.
He'd sleep in shelters; his nights were thick
and rigid, and they stifled him as if
they were made of ox-hide. He'd trail
dark-armed youths along the avenues,
sometimes successfully. He would have rather
taken them by force, his plunder claimed by right,
or seduced them with his guile, but he knew
they submitted out of pity. Then
he'd spend the night hours perched on the edge of the mattress,
moaning like someone sitting in the sand, the
skins' slaked lime still streaking his lips.
He quickly lost his job. He survived
on alms and petty theft.
Broken by hunger, he'd hallucinate naked
angels like glass or the eyes of certain fish.
We know he didn't make it to old age. Some
believe he died of starvation, but others
say it was in a knife fight with another beggar.

III

(THE CONFERENCE OF THE BIRDS)

In the middle of the Nasrid Palace is a
rectangular room, roofless, whose name
escapes me. Placid stone now dominating
no one, with a pond as brief
as a navel, like a single eye, like
a water-mouth mid-yawn. I sit on
the stairs, crushed by this heat that
hollows out the bones and carves them into flutes, surrounded
by tourists from Asia and Eastern Europe,
all frantic and overheated. Above
us, dozens of swifts cut across
the narrow air, cheeping, deafening the
walls and the clicking cameras and the hubbub,
sealing the entire summer with that single voice made
of knives, tiles, intangible ink, the wind's
tendons, as if trying to teach
a lesson, a revelation to the clammy
bodies that will wander here all afternoon and then
go home, show photos to their
families, and describe a building
ridden with birds—concluding, perhaps,
that the first man was not in fact
the first man, but barely a journey, a little
path grooved with blood and bile and marrow vivid
as sundown in August,
and that the first bird wasn't the first
bird, but a sound collected into the density
of flight, and that between the two is just
the headless clarity of this day. But maybe they
don't mean any of that. Maybe they're content
to fly from crack to crack, hovering up above,

where eternity is another untamed animal.
I sit there and the swifts and tourists pass me by.
Their happy calls are unbaptized children.

IV

(TÜBINGEN, SOME MONTH OR OTHER)

I've never been to Tübingen,
never walked along its rivers and its
houses. I couldn't tell you how to find
the tower where Hölderlin signed the poems
Celan would write much
later, in a German like
an abandoned swath of space, quarrelling
with time, a land of unexpected
enjambments, caesuras,
unsparing eyes. I never learned German,
don't have the passport that would let me
travel through that place of dazzled syllables,
founded by just two
people, this undeclared nation, realm
of contraband, whose shadows multiply
with every new translation. If I were stuck
in Tübingen, I wouldn't even be able to
pronounce its name, wouldn't know
how to say Tübin—
Tübin—
Tübingen.
The word would bite my tongue.
Crocodile word of unpredicted waters,
serpent of the seas going sleepily
to swamp, sonorous, under the palate.
Hungry word of mouths
articulating it. Tü-bin-
gen. Tü-bin-gen. Tü—
it coils behind the lips, lays
eggs in the darkness of saliva,
in the voice's restless nest. I've never

been inside this word, couldn't
tell you how to reach it, nor the tower,
nor the land that holds the poem
when all that's left is a destitute time.

V

Clipped nails, milk
teeth, skins diligently
stripped, amnesic dress, sweat,
the body's invisible ink,
the open syllable of menstrual
blood, dry semen turned
to salt-scar along the sheet.
This whole illegible account, oil
pooling deep down below
the days, heating up
furiously, viscous. The body's
testament amassed, fluid
and sickly spoils and vertebrae
half-set.
What's spent but never
measured. What rats
pilfer as we sleep,
crumbs and clots like
brief coagula fermented
in slumber. The skin, that slender water
we all sail with equal fear.

VI

(A NATURAL HISTORY OF DEBRIS: BONES)

Soon the blows stop hurting because
they fall in the same place, one after another, one
after another, and only resonate, bam bam bam
bam, like someone chopping wood in the
forest, someone you don't know, someone
who doesn't tell the trees his name before
he fells them. Bam bam bam bam: fist to
belly, ardently sinking in, belt against
the floor, back-handed slap, line of blood
sleepwalking down a forehead. That's what
happens to us, my siblings and me, nearly every day,
whenever something bothers him,
whenever his mood darkens. Sometimes
he takes out his revolver and shoots at the wall, at
the ceiling, to shut us up, so he can
sleep in peace. Then we go out onto
the porch and play with rusty tools,
shape dolls out of shovels
and hammers, hunt rats with sickles
because the rabbits are too fast
and Dad won't let us try it with his gun.
There are eight of us. We do what we can.
Once we even fashioned a sled out
of an old door. Dad called us idiots: here
it never snows. When I get bored, I
go to the pen in the backyard and talk
with the pigs we keep there. I tell them
stories, I tell them what I want to be
when I grow up, when I leave for the city.
Dad thinks I'm crazy; I think that's why he
hits me more than the others. Bam bam bam

bam. One day he went too far and that's how
I ended up here. I fell to the floor but didn't feel it.
I stopped breathing but didn't realize until later; sometimes
lifelong habits are broken in the strangest
ways. My eyes were shut
and even then I knew my dad was pacing
restlessly around me. Soon after
he carried me into the yard and left me
here, in the pen. The pigs began
to bite me. I wanted to tell them to stop, but
it really didn't hurt. Besides, Dad
almost never feeds them. When all the meat
was gone, they started on my bones.
They left a few so I could still
keep them company, telling them stories
so they wouldn't get sick of the heat and the mud.
When you die, you learn all sorts
of new words. Suddenly you know tales
you'd never heard before. The stories come from
far away, like the bam bam bam bam
of the blows on the rind of your skin, from very far
away, from places not even Dad
has been to, from people no one around
here has ever met. You also learn to listen
better when you're dead, when you don't
even have ears. That's how I heard
when Dad was on the news: officers
from the Kansas City police
department appeared in late November
at the residence of Michael A. Jones, age 44.
The police had received complaints
from the neighbors: shots were often
heard on Jones's property; it seemed
he beat his wife and children, one of whom
was missing. Soon after, many

men in uniform arrived and inspected
the house from top to bottom. They were slow
to check the corral. I didn't like what they did,
bothering my pigs, who hadn't done anything
wrong: they squealed when the officers dug up my bones.
Who would tell them stories now? Who
would tell them about all the things they'd never see? Don't
worry, I said, as they scooped me into
plastic bags, be patient, I'll be back soon.

VII
(ICELAND)

It took me years to discover that snow
is the least loving form of sleep.
I was slow to understand that
there's just more white behind its white,
a steady hunger that no one has ever
been able to draw, a furtive hand that thieves
unsuspecting passers-by when no one's watching.
I received this snow like someone presented with
the keys to an unbuilt house. And up above
all this atheist white is that prideless
sun, which cares for nobody.
At least the tropical sun watches over the thirst
that rasps our throats, gifts the metallic
sweat that fades our names and presses at
our foreheads with the weight of a promise. Here
the word "sun" reminds me of nothing. It doesn't
have a dazzling eye inside it, a sky
like a concave pupil. It trickles from my mouth, dries
uncomfortably at the corners of my lips. It doesn't
drag itself along the sky, doesn't wake me by banging
its clear hammer against the bell of my brain. Pale roofs,
streets stretching out to who knows where,
the password of coats and gloves—I still
haven't mastered these ways. I walk
carefully, like someone who half-hears voices and
gets confused, believing they speak
his language. It's always with me, this cold
like no one's bread.

VIII
(LITTLE ELEGY FOR SERGEANT SCHMIDT

A pocket-watch, gilt and out of fashion,
that sounded like the chattering of tiny teeth
if he brought it to his ear: that was the last
thing left intact in the jumble of flesh and
broken scaffolding that was Sergeant Schmidt.
It was the end of 1944 and the wall of a
building crushed him in Jarosław, during
the bombardment. The collapse snapped the stalk
of his spine, flimsy, blind. His organs
came apart like ripe fruit. Only then
did he understand that blood is made of
horses straining to run free. None
of his subordinates had time to gather
his remains. There was no morgue, no funeral; he went
into the mass grave, like countless others.
Above, the clouds gleamed like bones.
But all of this is speculation. I don't
know if his name was really Schmidt or his
rank a sergeant. I don't know if he belonged
to the Wermacht or the SS, if he stayed in Poland
the whole war, if he had children, a wife,
a lover, if he liked tea or coffee best, what
he thought of the clunking military boots, the yawning
panzer, the sound the roofs made when
they succumbed to exhaustion and let their ancient
backs cave in, if the smell of leather turned his stomach,
if he feared his superiors, if he knew some stupid
poem by memory, how many siblings he had,
whom he'd given insomnia, if he ever
learned that the dead go to the beach
at night to dance and drink

sweet guarapa, how many doors were in the house
where he was born, who taught him the words
he didn't dare use, or why he always dreamed
of dogs who licked his hands.
The only thing I know is that, in 1940,
during the occupation of Jarosław, an officer was
assigned to expel the residents at Number 4
Grodzka Street, command them to kneel
on the sidewalk, and execute them. Instead, he
ordered them to leave the city and flee toward
the Soviet border. It may have been the only
time he ever touched the sharp, fierce substance
of pity. The land of Nod is small; it fits
in a pocket. Its weight isn't always imperceptible.

IX

(IL MIGLIOR FABBRO)

It's a strange thing, a shadow. It belongs to the body, springs
out of it. It isn't made of the body's deaf
matter, but of its distance, its lack:
it's the body against the current. It appears
unbidden, when the light strikes us and demolishes
something inside us, something soundless
when it falls to the ground and stays there, humiliated. That's
why I prefer going out at night, when the sun
doesn't hang overhead like an ax or
a shout someone has sharpened, with that
clarity that makes you transparent and
uncovers all the badly-fitted scaffolding beneath
the skin, the crazy thicket of your veins.
When I can pay, I like going to some bar
or other. The Pullman, for example, on
Solano, especially for oldies night on Tuesday. I
sit at the bar, order a small bottle of beer, and
drink it sip by sip, making it last. Three is usually
my limit. We used to go to the ZZ or the Fragrata, and
we'd drink whiskey, when leaving after seven didn't make
us feel that cold sweat, dog sweat, biting at our backs.
My friends all died or left the country. They're
scribbles in my memory, the splinters
I leave wherever I go. Now I order a beer and drink
alone, because if you ask for Black Label in this joint
you get Vat 69. I go in and find
a spot where the light bulbs can't
exercise their stupidity and I can spy
on couples unobstructed. I don't attract anyone's
attention; who would want to hear my wrinkled
voice reciting the day's trifles,

how I write less and less because the letters
leap off the page like fleas and hide—
and then I spend all day scratching at
the bug-bites, see? Who would want that, right? I'm tired
of keeping words up at night.
So I sit in the Pullman and knead
the air. But this time someone
approached me. A thin boy, dark, thirty
tops. He touched my shoulder and smiled,
asked me to buy him a drink. Daniel Arnaldo, you've hit
the jackpot: he likes older guys, I guess.
Who knows what we talked about;
I've been forgetting things. I'm certain
I invited him over to my place and he said yes. I'm
sure of his hands on my skin, copying it,
his body under mine, sinking into the bed
like a fish seeking the depths. I must
have fallen asleep across our tired spit.
I'm sure of this, because I woke
to a noise. The boy was scoping the
room in a hurry. I sat up and called out to him. I couldn't
have said his name, because I didn't know it. He turned and
I saw he was holding a knife he must have found
in my kitchen. The light, the fucking morning light
shone onto him. And it was this radiance that he drove
quietly into my stomach. I don't think I reacted, or
even looked surprised; I hadn't yet found
my body on this side of wakefulness. I saw the gash,
and it didn't look like something that could happen to
a body. A misshapen mouth, a mouth with its lips
eaten away. I glanced around, disoriented, waiting for
something else to come out, not that rabid soup
I had inside me, but something else, expelled
from its hiding place, not knowing where to go.

X

My father had two births, but just
one life. On all the papers he'd zealously
collect as proof of his existence,
he'd written down a different date than the one
we always celebrated on his birthday. With
one of those dates, my father, weary,
was bribing death.

My sister and I would always ask him
to tell us about his childhood. He remembered
almost everything. The village, the houses,
his mother, his siblings—all intact. The
animals that shifted threateningly among
the trees, vague as someone else's
dream. Every leaf and its lineage, every fruit
and its warm, blind pulp. Near
the house was the river, rancor without end.

He disappeared on its banks for the first
time at five or six years old. He woke in the hot
gut of the wee hours and slipped out
undetected. The house was calm;
his steps must have been barely audible across
the thin twigs, splintered bones. He walked
in slumber, lids sealed shut with dust and wax. He
says they caught him at the edge, about to
fling himself into the current, looking for those fish
as spare as threads that someone tied together to escape.

In his stories, all things were marked by some
faulty gesture, as if disguised
as themselves. They were sheathed in

a sweet bark where moss had spread
over the years and ants cleared imperceptible
paths. His own father barely let himself
be remembered. His traits had gone astray; perhaps
he'd lost them in a foolish bet, or he wasn't
a man at all, just a presence whose density
and volume defied measurement, a rage, some
knuckles, a brutal headless lust. He hung inert
in the middle of my father's memory, like
that bull he saw when he was small, suspended
face-down, white-eyed, open-throated, as
the soft clay of his blood spilled into a pot.

People used to say I had my father's hands.
I don't know if he also had his father's. But maybe
they have mine. Maybe I'm the one
who lent them; maybe I'm marking them now
with every gesture, every fold.
We have to read legacy backwards, travel it
with our fingers as if deciphering the uneven
punctuation of Braille. Sailing upward: fashioning
a ship out of the body's own sad wood.

XI

(INTENSIVE BIOPOLITICS COURSE 2)

Today, major newspapers report,
a group of businessmen, in cooperation with
the Greater Caracas Mayoralty, has just
founded a company that offers
intimate tours around the city for
a modest price. Nostalgic émigrés and curious
tourists will be able to investigate the wildest parts
of the metropolis and make contact with its native
inhabitants from an armored van driven by an armed
professional. The vehicle will be
provisioned with food and drinks of
the highest quality, as well as the products
of our corporate sponsors. After signing a
series of authorization forms, the explorers will
participate in excursions to the mouth
of the Guaire, our Ganges, and will have the chance
to photograph the exotic fauna perched on rooftop
terraces or peering out of windows
with eyes like pools of tense
water. Various prominent politicians (on both
the left and right) have already booked
their tickets. In a playful tone, the pamphlet
promises adventurers that the journey will
reveal "the nimble, almost tender
mechanisms of mercy." Immediately
thereafter, it advises participants to
refrain from reaching their hands out
of the vehicle during the ride, as well as from feeding
any residents of Caracas, as their bodies are
no longer used to certain items. Guests are also
asked to remain silent or speak

softly, because isolation has convinced
the city's populace that their language
is the only one spoken in the world; a string
of unfamiliar sounds could scare them off. Plus,
the document adds, then they'll be able to hear
"the whispers exchanged by Venezuelans
when they think no one is watching, a crumbling
sound, like an old bill passed from hand
to hand." In TV interviews, numerous celebrities have
declared their interest in visiting these extraordinary
places, coated by the sun: a drop of oil.

XII

(LEIBNIZ, MON AMOUR)

In one possible world, trees
weigh less than the sum of their leaves,
time is measured in blinks, and people
spend long spells every night unstitching
light for dawn to break. Anthropophagy
has become the only acceptable form of love.
But only in the best of all possible
worlds live those who stay awake all
night, trying to figure out how to make death
sentences more efficient, less tedious for the living.
They've even written out a list of their objections:

1. The electric chair uses too much energy. The
buildings around the prison lose power
during executions. Nearby residents complain
about the smoke and the smell of burnt flesh.

2. The firing squad wakes the neighbors. Some
have even leaned out of their windows, guns
in hand, to fire back.

3. The guillotine requires disinfectants, chlorine,
janitorial services. The budget is too tight
to hire so large a staff.

4. The executioner almost never finds the vein
on his first try. Lethal injections take
too long to work: the convict suffers
for hours, causing all sorts of marketing
and HR headaches. Besides, the drugs
tend to vanish mysteriously from the warehouse.

People know they're clumsy in this world. Which is why
many demand the soothing crack
of the trachea snapping on the gallows: face
swollen and deformed, thick tongue protruding.
They bury the executed with stones in their throats
so they won't protest. They sleep serenely, because
they don't fully understand how death does its business,
what it requests in exchange for its services, how
it refuses to be domesticated or tell anyone its name—
because it can't, because its name is a continual and indefinite
series of points stretched out along a plane, nothing more.

XIII

We travel: space is what foretells us.
If there were a god watching over us, a
god of transit, detours, forks
in the road, then it must be a tiny
god. Staring out the window of
the train, at how the buildings slip away,
startled children running, I imagine that god whose
name would be a mystery because he'd accidentally
left it in the seat-back pocket of a plane.
He'd have no rites or temple, would offer neither
solace nor proof, would be elected by no tribe. No one
would devote their words to him in matins
or at meals; his prayers would be blank dawns
spent in bus stations or airports,
his breathing muddied with the rain falling
in his bronchial tubes at that time of day. He wouldn't talk
with other gods, who don't exist, either.
He'd barely sing his song to whoever would go with him.
He wouldn't punish theft or adultery: he'd know
that every path is a theft, every word
an adultery. He'd have too many children to choose
one to wash away our sins. Instead,
he'd force us to migrate, as if he could absolve
distance of its vastness, of its fear.
We'd walk so much that he could only
recognize us from a distance. His only purpose would
be to make sure the clocks still worked,
so that departures could happen, so that eternity
couldn't seep in here. He'd be the god of
delayed flights, shuttered ticket booths, the stench
of piss and sleeping semen in public restrooms.
He'd make a body out of me, just one among many, without

the torment of abstraction. He'd exchange my eyes
for bitter coals, turn my hands to distant
animals. He'd reduce me to the ravenous
geometric certainty of motion. He'd show me that wakefulness
is not a state, but a task of destruction.

XIV
(STRANGE FRUIT)

It's common knowledge: fish don't talk. They cut quietly
across the sea's inverted sky, suspended
like other people's thoughts, hung against the open-
mouthed night. It's said they don't sing because
they fear their voices will escape, dart up to the surface,
and float there, sleeping the slumber
of algae. Pierre de Vaisière recounts that in June 1724
a slave ship crossed these stagnant voices
bound for Santo Domingo. Its hull was stocked with canned
goods, fresh water, rats, cats to hunt them,
and and three hundred humans to be sold. It smelled of tedium
and dysentery, of piled-up bodies, lapped by niter. Halfway
through the journey, the captain started to suspect that two
slaves, a man and a woman, were planning a mutiny. To hedge
his bets, he decided to make an example of them. Before
the whole ship, the captain made his men peel off the skin
of her limbs with a knife; when she died, her bones were hoarse
from all the shouting. After slashing her throat, he ordered them
to pull out the man's heart, liver, and innards, then cut them into
exactly two hundred ninety-eight pieces. His arms and legs hung
open, exposed, swaying back and forth with the shifting of
the ship. Revealing the tremulous tree he
harbored, where the sky's red roots sank in.
Each slave received a sliver, flesh
of their lost flesh. They closed their mouths as
the sea closed around the ship, throatless,
lipless, gumless. The bodies were tossed
overboard. And then received by fish that, in truth,
don't speak because they're deaf. They saw the bodies fall and didn't
dare interrogate the blank eyes, the flayed
skin, the viscera suddenly free. The fish didn't ask
their names, and that's why we don't know them, either.

XV
(NATURAL HISTORY OF DEBRIS: HEADS)

The head of John the Baptist sculpted by Rodin
in 1887 kisses the plate it rests on, as if
it were a mirror or a window through which he
could glimpse the other side of wakefulness. Not one
more blessing hangs from his lips: he's tired of speaking.
Now he chooses his words with care, but needs
someone else to extract them from his mouth, where
they're hidden, holding their breath. The sea shines
in his marbled white hair.

*

Frederick Wilhelm Murnau was born in 1888 and died in
1931. In late 2015, his body was exhumed and
his skull removed from a cemetery near
Berlin. The authorities believe that thieves disfigured
the body for some sort of ritual. But
that fleshless face can only tell them about the barely
audible sound made by worms devouring meat
when they perform their ancient sacramental task. And about
the silence after, the sand housed in fissures and hollowed
sockets, every grain a dot of untamed
night. Boredom is the only thing that resembles
eternity: it labors with an honest love for detail.

*

Contrary to the tales about the incident, when
they dismembered his body and scattered his limbs,
they didn't fling his head into the river. They decided to keep it
on a makeshift altar, and there it stayed for years,

pale and swollen, eyes empty, dark dried blood
where the throat should have begun.
People traveled from far and wide to see it, to ask it
questions; they hoped it would prophesy or sing, offer
riddles like coins from a country no one
has ever been to. Almost blurry, the head of
Orpheus sings no songs, but that doesn't mean
it has no marvels to grant: from the corner of its
lips emerges, day and night, a strand of stubborn spittle.

XVI

The roar of passing airplanes strikes
the building in the forehead. I'm watching
Bugs Bunny convince a hunter that he isn't
a rabbit. The air is pale at nine
a.m., fine as a communion wafer. My four
years on this earth fit with their full weight
on the chair in front of the TV. When the planes
slice across the sky, scratching it, everything shakes,
all infected by a single shudder, as if
the world had suddenly decided to expose
its guts. Everyday geography had been
submissive: no apparitions, no marvels. No one
loaned us their miracles, and in any case we didn't
have enough to buy one. But that morning some
planes destroyed the sound barrier right
above my head, above my tangled, sleepy
hair. The sky's dislocated jaw
let out a ragged cry, a single
word made entirely of stones. Then there was
nothing on the screen, just some multicolored bars
and an insistent whistle that seemed to want to pierce
my eardrum. I ran to the window to see what was happening
and my father made me duck below the sill. Then
I heard the shots: one, two, three, immaculate. I'm not
sure about the bullet shattering that window
in our apartment in Quinta Crespo: I may have
made it up. But that broken glass was
the first layer of what would one day be my skin.
This scene is all I have; the story would come
later. It's the shoddy photomontage of childhood, an arrhythmia
of images faded with use, blurred because
it always rains in memories. The water

scrapes the surface of the photos as if trying
to seep into them. Swamp them. Flood them.

XVII

I have studied the science of goodbyes,
the bare-headed laments of night.
Osip Mandelstam

In Nataruk, in northern Kenya, archaeologists
discovered the remains of 27 human beings
heaped into the dry palm of what
was once a lake. According to the carbon
dating of shells and mineral sediment,
the bodies were somewhere between 9,500
and 10,500 years old. It was a varied
group: adult men and women
(one pregnant), elders, children.
Several had their hands still bound. All
bore marks of severe injury, signs
of blunt trauma, like club-blows, and lacerations
caused by sharp objects. Experts
believe the 27 individuals were
subdued, summarily executed, and
thrown into the lake, where the silt endeavored
to preserve them. This is how bodies
learn to talk, to utter life un-
eloquently, in pounds of flesh, bile,
phlegm, spit, dust, and inclement sheen.
Life with parted lips and rotted
teeth, bones gone to lead. Hide stretched
under the midday fury, eye brusque and
hollowed out. Disappearance, valediction,
phantom limb, science cut short.

XVIII
(DUBIA ET SPURIA)

Fr. 54

Many years later, as he faced
the firing squad, he was to remember that distant
afternoon when his father, foaming at
the mouth, came to blows with a man in the village
bar, hauled him out to the street, and beat him to a pulp.
The little reddened teeth
gleamed on the ground, scattering like startled ants.

*

Fr. A 3

Every night, Persephone buys a ticket
at the Franklin Avenue / Botanic Garden Station and
spends hours riding the subway. One of her eyes
can only see what has already been; the other betrays her
by making her see what can never be. She hasn't yet determined
if it's the left or the right. She rides in hope
that some stranger will approach and offer her a pomegranate.

*

Fr. D 7

One day, the occupying forces disappeared.
No planes or helicopters passed overhead; there was no noise
of trucks departing. The camp was left
intact: arms, ammunition, vehicles, uniforms,
provisions, all cached away with something

like modesty. Months later, we discovered that
they'd found a way to fulfill their mission:
under the fields and haciendas, feeding the
earth, the trees, the grass, those soldiers
rotted rabidly. It was too late.

*

Fr. 27

Many years later, as he faced the firing squad,
he was to remember that distant afternoon when his father
took him to the brothel. The girls waved from a distance.
Two were still marked with the bruises he had
left them. There was no ice in the village to reduce the swelling.
He, still a child, let himself be led, but he couldn't have sex with
any of them. Desire was a scratch that festered on his skin, that filled
his throat with an unfamiliar liquid. He was mute,
paralyzed. Mockery and ridicule awaited him at home.

*

Fr. E 9

...unburied, subjected to the buzzards' lust.

*

Fr. C 31

Everyone cheered when the king's head
tumbled across the floor, detached from his body by
the tidy passion of the guillotine. After a couple weeks
had passed, however, a rumor spread: the king had
another head hidden away somewhere. Some

said it was in the palace; others conjectured
that it must be concealed among the talking relics
at the cathedral. But one thing was for sure: wherever it was,
everyone insisted, the king still reigned.

*

Fr. A 14

Charon sits on this side of the river
and smokes. The dead throng
around him—standing up, because they've forgotten
how to sit. The boatman refuses
to take them. He won't accept bottle
caps or empty beer cans
for his services.

*

Fr. 32

Many years later, as he
faced the firing squad, he was to
remember that distant afternoon when
his father took him to hunt deer for
the first time. He was a good shot despite his
maimed left hand—people say
he was born with six fingers, but one
fine day he grabbed a knife and severed
the extra digit. He taught his son how
to flay, how to remove the
guts and store the blood. He kept
the deer's eyes for himself. No way
of knowing what he'd do with them.

*

Fr. A 33

The night the president died, not
a single person noticed. The palace's other
inhabitants were drinking, watching porn, or simply
sleeping. It wasn't until the next day that they found
his body, already distended, like a sponge
that would have stored whatever was left of
the night inside him. After the obligatory shouts
and weeping, the appropriate
prayers, they closed his eyes. Which instantly
snapped open. His kinsfolk and
companions didn't flinch: they shut his eyes
again. And an instant later they
were open once more. And so they spent the first
half of the day waging this lopsided battle with
the hallowed lids. They called for ministers, aides,
representatives from the chamber of entrepreneurs, even
the senior military officers—no one knew what to do.
They couldn't bury him that way. Finally,
the vice-president had an idea: he suggested they replace
his eyes and lids with false ones. And so they did.

*

Fr. 15

Many years later, as
he faced the firing squad, he
was to remember that distant
afternoon when his father
showed him the novel he'd
been writing for years,

a book to preserve
the sum of what he'd forgotten.

*

Fr. C 5

To live life so that it's left
intact when we leave it,
so that someone else can pick it up
off the ground, stretch it out, dust it off, wear
it loose. To drink our water, yawn
away our boredom, laugh at our second-
hand ironies. As far as life is concerned, continuity
and plagiarism are one and the same.

*

Fr. E 2

...of all crafts learned,
just...nakedness.

*

Fr. 11

Many years later, as he faced the firing squad, he was
to remember that distant afternoon when his father lay dense
and swollen on his deathbed. He retained water as he did
everything else, with the same rage; he didn't want a single drop
left over in this world. Delirious, he was convinced that thirst
would demolish all the houses in the village within days, drive the horses
mad, devour the cows from inside. There was no one to take care
of him; no one could stand him. He'd been kicked out by the mayor

and his other children had fled to the capital. That night, once
they'd moved his body, they found two bags under the bed, like garbage
bags, full of chicken bones, faded photographs,
bullets, and a bottle of rotgut, unopened.

XIX
(NATURAL HISTORY OF DEBRIS: KIDNEYS)

Patient Name: Adalber Salas Hernández
ID Number: ■■■ ■■■■ ■■■■
Age: 21
Weight: 63.5 kg
Height: 173 cm
Referred by Dr. ■■■■■ ■■■■■■
The patient reports severe lumbar pain on the right side, radiating to the epigastrium, thorax, and back (shoulder), over the past 15 days, intensifying with deep inhalation. He came to the emergency room and was found to have ESRof 52 mm, 2+ protein in urine, urinary casts (0-4 per field), and negative urine cultures, with proteinuria at 2.93 g/24 h. Several days later, he presented an induration with limited function in the dorsal vein of the right elbow, with mild edema without erythema.

[Needles demarcating the space between the
ribs, the opaque expanse of this region
where there are no houses, where cattle don't
graze, where no tree stretches into the cold of its
branches. Needles working the ribs
as if engraving them, their curve
embracing the lungs' rich silt.]

Medical history:
Childhood asthma.
No known drug allergies.
Extraction of three wisdom teeth on May 21, 2009. Took ibuprofen every 12 hours, diclofenac every 6 hours, and clindamycin every 10 hours.
Resection of the nasal conchae and correction of deviated septum.
Intense febrile episode in November.
Vaccinated against hepatitis.

[Moss growing on the fleshy walls,
in the tunnels, biting at the scaffolding
of the breath. Algae in
the pleura's light pool, climbing
tenaciously. A cough
like a hungry dog, barking,
snapping at the bronchi.]

Family medical history:
Father: Living, age 55, labyrinthitis.
Mother: Living, 51, dyslipidemia, osteoporosis.
Siblings: 1S APS.
Family history of diabetes.
HPB: Prior tobacco smoking, denies current consumption, three cups of coffee daily, alcoholic beverages every three days approx. Medications: marijuana, hashish.
Rest of physical exam presents no variations.

[Organ artifacts eaten away with use,
whittled with wear, suspended.
Among them, the tautological
language of the blood, veins
tensed to measure distances
we don't suspect.
A layer of plaster forms
over them, bit by bit.

Organs that hang from their minimal
insomnia, that don't sleep or permit sleep.]

Diagnosis:
Nephrotic syndrome.
Membranous glomerulonephritis (stage I-II).
The possibility of secondary membranous glomerulonephritis must be ruled out. The patient will be referred for upper and lower GI endoscopy.

He will also be referred for a percutaneous renal biopsy.

[Organs like fish that swim
in blind water. Creatures without
witnesses, living far from the
rabid empire of the gaze.
They fear discovering the coast of this
subterranean sea, its naked
and dazzled shore, zenithal knife.
Beyond the skin, the light:
the most finished form of fear.]

Treatment:
Losartan potassium: 50 mg daily.
Omega-3: two capsules daily.
Prednisone: 30 mg at 8 a.m. and 30 mg at 4 p.m.
Mycophenolate mofetil: 1 gr every 12 hours.
Warfarin: 5 mg daily.
Omeprazole: 40 mg daily.
The treatment will be adjusted according to the results of monthly checkups.

[The body's coral silence.]

XX

Last Sunday morning, according to
the National Directorate of Forensic
Sciences, the entire staff of the Colinas
de Bello Monte morgue suddenly left
the facilities of said institution.
Witnesses state that some employees
shouted or ran off haphazardly. Some
time later, that same day, CICPC officials
appeared in front of the building, accompanied
by distinguished experts and professors from
the Medical School of the Central University of
Venezuela, and by a coronel from the National
Guard, two psychics, a young priest, an old priest,
and five babalaos. After spending some time inside the morgue,
they struggled through the doors and stated
before this and other media outlets: during the
night, the recently admitted corpses had
come back to life and declared their intention
to substantiate their status as citizens of
the Republic. On that day and the ones
that followed, similar events were reported
in all Venezuelan cemeteries and forensic
facilities. Since then, the dead have slowly
been assembling, docile and hollow-eyed. Sparing
no efforts or resources, they have managed to found
a non-profit organization, the Agency for the
Protection and Development of Decomposing
Bodies, the APDDB. Through a campaign of
marches and peaceful demonstrations,
they seek the official recognition of their
civil rights and the establishment of a permanent
seat in the National Assembly.

The President has expressed his approval,
ordering the immediate creation of the Ministry
of Popular Power for Posthumous Relations. The church,
aside from revoking a couple papal bulls, has said
nothing. Numerous religious cults have proclaimed the end of
the world, but the dead themselves seem fairly
bored by the idea. A few eminent politicians have
expressed their concerns to the press:
how can a body with a rotted tongue,
with a chest eaten away by silent worms, have
rights? Although only a week
has passed since these occurrences began, the
APDDB has released a statement
informing the national population (with a detectable
pulse) that the dead refuse to close their eyes, to
be written into the book of disappearances.
Commencing with the phrase "Corpses of the
world, unite!," this document urges
the living to recognize their worth as members of
this nation and to accept them as valuable ("vital"
is the term of choice) to the community. It
addresses the afterlife in detail, describing it as an
impoverished, overpopulated place, a third-rate
tourist destination where lost souls are forced
to wait in endless lines to acquire even basic
goods. Given the exorbitant devaluation
of eternity, it is all but impossible to buy
anything with the empire's currency: the teeth
you carry with you at the moment of
your death. Likewise, the statement
lists a series of demands that the corpse
community is setting to the residents
of mortal life. These include
the censorship of zombie movies (considered
prejudicial and a lightning rod

for hatred) as well as an adjustment
to Spanish-language spelling norms:
the addition of two new accents on
the word cadáver, now written as
cádávér, with three neat cuts or three
bullet wounds, a term they feel
will represent the group
more fairly. At a press release
convened to present the statement, the leader
of the APDDB implied that one of
them may throw his hat in the ring for
the next presidential elections. According to the latest
surveys, experts say, the country
may soon be governed by a corpse.

XXI

The noise returns every night, around
three, three-thirty a.m. Soft clicks, scratches, the sound
of tiny breaking bones. The rats
converse behind the wall. I never
see them; I only hear them move and labor
in the intravenous darkness that mediates between
my apartment and my neighbor's. I
sense them traveling to and fro, frenetic,
roaming that provisional geography, building
tunnels, depots, corridors, a tubular city,
a circulatory nocturnal system. And all
the while, that language. Rats have tongues
made of plastic and sawdust, of lumps
and words they've spent centuries filching,
words we haven't uttered ever since.
Words from all the languages ever spoken.
Which is why it doesn't matter where we are; the shrieks
of rats always sound like childhood memories.

The artisans of expiration are
alone. No one has ever bothered
to preach to them, convert them to this faith or that.
We don't know if they believe in the existence of the soul or if
they think we deserve one. We do know, however,
that they bury their dead beneath our mattresses.

They don't let us see them. Still, every
morning, I find signs in the corners, testimonies
in the form of trim little feces, elongated as
calligraphy. They may be excerpts from
individual memoirs, or the anonymous history of the whole
collective, a story that stretches from the

creation of the world until the end of time, the last
dirty kitchen, the last garbage can. Or maybe
these tiny heaps of shit, so meticulously
arranged, are the lament of some
rat driven to desperation because flesh
is sad and it's read all the books there are.

When I sleep, I dream that one of them, the same
one every time, climbs up onto the bed and skitters onto
my chest. My torso gapes open: with nervous teeth,
the rat peers right into my lungs. It
examines them carefully, sniffs them, and
is gone, trailing its naked tail along
the sheets. There it leaves them, exposed, inflated,
two sacks of air and lukewarm anticipation.

XXII

The language I speak is made of faulty
questions, of cropped, repeated phrases.
Every day, it hammers on my door, demanding
food, and threatening to knock my teeth out.
It's not really sure where it comes from, and it doesn't
care: mother tongue, father tongue,
what does it matter.

It teeters in on crutches and fills the house with dirt.
It has no table manners and never smiles
when I complain. My language
is merciless with me. It visits me because
it's tired, because it needs a meal, a bed.
It comes in, sprawls out, and ignores me; it befriends
the mice, the ants, the cockroaches skittering away
to hide in the corners, under the furniture. It gathers up
its stories, sketches them in the dust with a skinny
finger, beside the flowerpots brimming with half-
smoked cigarettes.

My language has neither sacraments
nor miracles. It thinks it needs them to conceal
its nakedness, but that isn't true. And it thinks
the feel of its own flesh is all
the prayer it needs, its own heft pulling
us toward the sleeping center of the earth.

It's obsessed with the scandalous exactitude
of hunger, with how it slowly disassembles us,
how it scours us for our bones.
It would like to get rid of itself, to be graffiti or
a billboard or a scrawl in fresh

cement. It would like to curse and rail and swear with
propriety, but that's just not its forte, either.

My language has never been able to resemble
itself. It's made of words that say
goodbye as soon as they arrive. In it,
all forms are dazzled bodies,
all things buckle as if the light
were going to wring them out. It speaks impatiently
and stares at me. And in that moment we're
the only two inhabitants of a continent surrounded
by waters that never sleep.

XXIII
(NATURAL HISTORY OF DEBRIS: LAZARUS)

First came the breath falling furious
onto the waters. A few words half-
heard, raucous stones hurled
against the pane of sleep. He's always struggled
to get up in the morning. Defying all of death's codes,
unfamiliar hands grab Lazarus by the shoulders and
drag him into the midday light, abrupt as a
cliff. They pry open his mouth and force in bitter
breath, thump his chest until
his heart revs up again, until the body's
gutters fill once more with the forgetful,
bloody torrent, motor oil, diesel
fuel. He stumbles his way out of the sepulcher, blinded
by the glare; he's lost his shroud, and
the witnesses to the miracle can see his flesh
darkened by putrefaction, striped with worms,
the map of another world. The stench is overpowering.
All cover their noses; some vomit. Lazarus
blinks in the stubborn radiance, his dry
gaze burns, he can't focus it. No one understands
why he's been brought back to the world, but
the newspapers are thrilled. A documentary
is in the works, plus a reality
show (Lazarus and six young people in a house,
learning to surf or cooking in front of an audience).
His photo is all over Twitter, #loosehimandlethimgo.
Astrologists squabble over the birth
chart of someone twice born. He keeps
blinking. He gestures, stammers, drops
his syllables, clumsy toys. Groans, grunts. How
to fire up the voice's soft machine again.

The witnesses soon disperse. Lazarus is
left alone, still at a loss for how to clothe his naked body,
starting to understand that god is a blind muscle.
Finally, he takes a sidelong glance and walks away and that's the end of it.

XXIV

Gummy, semi-transparent gloves, bladeless
scalpel, face mask, oversized white
robe. I'm fifteen years old and in the lab,
in biology class, surrounded by tiny animals in
jars of formaldehyde, plastic anatomical
models and precision instruments that no one
has ever used. Every week, a hanging skeleton
observes us from its corner as we struggle
to understand the graceless, viscous secret kept
by living bodies. Today I had to bring in a cow's
heart. I hauled its blackened, greasy weight around all
morning long, packed in a cooler so it wouldn't
rot. I've lugged it patently. Now
it's on the counter, laid out on the dissection
table. It doesn't tremble when I open it,
cutting through the fatty tissue as best I can,
enduring the murky funk that clings to my throat.
Elastic fibers, membranes, atria, ventricles,
all resisting my touch, places where a rough
flower grew, a cold and anxious ground that's no
one's motherland. This is where the blood ran, conveying
its belongings, its concrete contraband, through
the pulmonary valve, and then the aortic,
which groaned thickly, straining as the liquid passed.
An enormous instrument, atrocious, flesh
and tense fat clenched with rage, fold
upon fold, just like mine, hidden in
the chest's amniotic darkness, among the springs,
cogs, and tattered cables of the thoracic cage,
far from the bitter border of all things, pulsing
like a galaxy sunk into the distance,
whose light erodes and ages

before it ever reaches us. The device's only virtue
was its blindness; here, in the purgatory of the
table, between the body it was wrested from and
the mute paradise of halogen bulbs,
it's exposed, diminished, bringing to our sight
the passageways traveled by the inarticulate
voice that once nursed us all,
the same that fed us the hoarse
mud of life. Now, it's quiet, stilled of rhetoric,
mere scaffolding, a crossing point. It learned that distance
is measured not in meters but in vanishings. That I
is not an other; that I is nobody, a chain of piled-up
throbs, noise, rust, prosody un-possessed by anyone.

XXV
(NATURAL HISTORY OF DEBRIS: AUSCHWITZ-BIRKENAU)

When not a single person I remember is still here, when not
a single stalk of our memory still stands tall and our voices
aren't worth their weight in salt or ash or spices, what
will these buildings look like? As the Allied pilots found them
with their cameras: slow lines of rectangles embracing
the snow, ribs burgeoning in the hungry air?
Or as I see them on Google Earth: barracks
gleaming like skulls, gates and wires with clean,
almost courteous barbs, all a little sleepy, feigning
the innocence of abandoned objects under the dry
membrane of my screen? Seen from the sky, the earth
is smooth, impermeable, bulimic. It's ageless, or perhaps
it's as old as the myths forgotten because they're no longer useful
to anyone. Someone will observe all this with neither
curiosity nor terror, with pupils veiled by the resin of distance, as if
the past couldn't be the future and time was just
the country of what has already been seen. When we find
ourselves chewing at the guts of the ground and we don't
have the cloth of a name to cover up our nakedness, we won't be able
to warn them that history is one long curfew in which
no one ever really gets a full night's sleep.

XXVI

We were all afraid of sleeping under
the same roof as my mother. In the middle
of the night, as we slumbered, her shouts
would jolt us awake. I've never heard
anyone else scream that way: like
a tearing, an incandescence, something yanked
out of an animal womb. Every night, she'd exhaust
her vocal cords; she'd wake up hoarse, her voice
cracked and porous. She'd yell like someone splitting
open a skull with her bare hands, smashing it
against a rock.

A few months passed and the blank
shrieks were joined by laughter, grunts,
and dance steps. Eyes closed, gestures blurred,
my mother would crinkle up her face, bare her teeth
furiously, shake her head, or swing her arms,
trying to shoo away one of those birds that only
flies on the other side of wakefulness. When she laughed,
her limbs would stretch and flex, tensed with
effort. Her bursts of laughter were a shattered window.
She'd stay in bed

for the rest of the night, her
body narrowing until she became a shrunken
form, a geological formation whetted over
years of quiet waiting. She was like those
people buried in Pompeii: she had the same
urge to transform herself into a stone among stones,
the same mineral anatomy. Fixed to her chest, a closed
fist: it clenched the nodule that had grown
in my grandmother's left breast,
a prop-heart, a replacement organ. There
she stored her dirty cough, her hospital visits,

her pills, her sleepless nights, all sedimented now
beneath the calcified skin of sleep.

XXVII
(ANABASIS)

A bus in the middle of the highway. That's how this ends.
Behind it, abandoned, out of gas, is a military transport
van riddled with bullet holes. The day we left,
we stuffed all the clothes we could fit in our packs and
bags. We took some jewelry and packed that too; we
hid the rest behind the refrigerator, surmising that
we'd have a need for it someday. Money
tucked into socks and underwear. My daughter taped a letter
to the kitchen door, asking the next arrivals
not to break anything, please. The portraits, family
photos—the ants will carry them away, she told me when
we left the building. They're going to crumble all our stuff to bits,
a little at a time, and store it in their secret cities. My brother
had a contact, someone who could get us a spot
on one of the boats, absolutely, no question, as certain
as the weight of a peach or the smell of bread on the table
in the morning. For a price, of course. We paid it. The bus
we boarded was pulled over twice, once as we were just exiting
the city, but they didn't make us get off. Inside,
no one said a word: the horizon ran its razor blade along
our tongues. We were alert to the brakes' intestinal squeal,
letting the heat digest us, slowly, over the plastic lining
of the seats. Sometimes I rested my head against
the back and tried to imagine what we must look like
from afar, moving down the empty highway, suturing
the distance that kept us from the coast. I don't remember who
once told me that the ocean didn't even seem like water;
it looked more like an enormous sheet of paper creased by some
distracted hand. But that's what I'm thinking now. When we saw
the shore, flimsy, there, all I thought was: sea. And we said: sea.
Which was like saying boundless eyelids. Which was like saying

hunger. Which was like saying time's saliva. Which was
like saying the dead's interminable hair. Which was like
saying terror. The sea was the biggest startled animal we
had ever seen. We were advancing toward it when
we heard the shots. The van was up ahead, soldiers
firing at who knows who, tiny figures, still remote.
The driver stepped on the gas. He wanted to cut through
the crossfire at top speed, we couldn't stop, we didn't know what
they might do to us. Without ever ordering us to halt, without
a single gesture, they pumped the bus with bullets. The driver braked
at once. Soon, when the detonations were over,
they came for us. They took all the women
and killed all the men. And then they fled, not glancing
down at what they'd done. They left us scattered here, the salt
of the earth. That's how a bus ends up in the middle of
highway, in the dead of night, sad as a dog in heat.

XXVIII

Simple words: rain, sun, house, tree, road, mother,
father, brother, laughter, now, animal, fear. Simple
and dependable as fingers. Complex words: name,
number, blow, shout, question, bullet, accusation, past,
future, patience, animal, fear. When I was little,
I often went to the natural history museum. It was a
large, white building with a portico invaded by
faux Doric pillars facing a circular courtyard. Through
the entrance, on the right, was a wing devoted
to the planet's geological eras. Layers of
earth like shut eyelids, impossibly far-off
countries, sleeping forever beneath our feet.
Places and periods I couldn't fluently pronounce,
all christened just so that the distance
wouldn't burn our hands. The earth
hoarded lives, shed skins with impunity;
fossils were left as proof, obscene as Polaroids
of a world that has nothing to say to us.
A little deeper in, a whole wing was devoted
to the animal kingdom. Encased behind quavering
displays, all kinds of specimens watched people
walk past with glass eyes. The skins of their dead
bodies had been meticulously removed, salted,
rehydrated, tanned. Once dried and muted, without
the idiotic murmur of their vital fluids corralled
inside them, they'd been arranged in crowded frames.
Birds of prey perched on plastic and foam rubber
branches that grew and lengthened out of time, beasts
with yellow fangs and carious pelts, distracted
herbivores, stagnating in endless poses, grazing,
standing guard, hunting, being hunted, caught
in the deaf mimicry of desire. I'd move with caution,

back to the wall, both terrified and curious,
softly repeating all the simple words I could
remember. The throng of fauna made me hope I'd run
into a stuffed angel at any moment: my grandmother
had told me they were God's own beasts of burden.
But I'd never make it to the end of the hall. There weren't
enough simple words in the world, not enough to buy
my passage from one of fear's levees to another. I'd leave
just as carefully, trying not to draw attention to myself,
to keep from disturbing that cold somnambulism. I've
never returned as an adult. Those animals tamed by chemical
preservatives told me what they had to: a poem is a predator
that has been hunted, flayed, and tenderized, whose flesh
is gone, whose skin is fixed, menacing and ridiculous,
to a skeleton of simple and complex words.

XXIX

So you want to write a love
poem. Here's some advice:

don't write too much. Love, when brief,
is twice as loving. No one wants confessions
or obscenities these days: social media and porn
sites have monopolized the market
of intimacy. Consider erotic haiku instead.

Form is everything. But you don't want some complicated
gizmo, some obsolete machine. Sonnets,
romances, couplets—they all smell a little
like that tuna fillet that's been hidden away in the fridge
for weeks. You want a latest-model
poem, a convertible, bright with tweetable lines, that
fits as neatly into teenage jerk-off sessions as
into the fists of domestic abusers.

(This space serves as a practice room
for love poems' presumptuous gymnastics.)

Some love poems are downright fat.
They're anxious eaters; not a jot of self-control. Their
nervous, greasy fingers can't stop handling adjectives
and similes. They press against the page, against the eyelids.
Doctors warn them that if they don't lose weight, if they don't
start exercising, they could develop diabetes or a
cardiac condition. But there's nothing sadder than
a voluminous, proparoxytone love poem
picking at a salad.

(Time, like them, is prone to choking fits
because it wants to eat too much.)

Don't skimp on coral lips, pearl teeth, emerald
eyes: they're vintage accessories that will soon
be back in style. The beloved
face is a playing field (make sure you repeat this
to yourself when you wake up every morning): its nooks
and folds deserve metaphors of the foulest
lineage, the most brilliant piercings.

If the poem's nakedness is unbearable, if
you can't stand its skinny arms, its twisted
limbs, its gaunt and cross-eyed stare, then dress it up
with an epigraph. Find yourself a brand-name
supplier and make sure you get your products
in the right size. Don't buy where Jaime
Sabines or Joaquín Sabina did. There's good reason not to.

Be selective with your clientele. There are love poems for
whetting the appetite, love poems for improving
circulation, love poems for weathering the
winter, love poems for washing dishes
and scouring saucepans, love poems sold
like laxatives, love poems for after
love, love poems for clearing up acne, love
poems that cure the common cold, love poems that
dispense with alcoholism (or inspire it, depending).

Try to remember a couple things. Your love poem
won't rectify any injustice, or refine anyone's
sensibility, or feed the hungry, or quench
a thirst, or overturn a death sentence. Your
love poem won't earn you so much as a cent
of love: at most, it might help some asshole convince
his girlfriend that he won't ever hit her
again.
        (All love poems are accomplices
to violence.)

If you're lucky, it'll land someone
a quickie some night—that and nothing
more. But don't be discouraged: the love poem
market has been losing ground to Viagra
and other Sildenafil-based drugs for decades
now. It's never too late for a career change.

XXX
(A DAY IN THE LIFE)

Before his alarm goes off, the government
minister's eyes are already open: he gets out of bed
with the hoarse creaks of the ironworks hidden
behind his ribs. He brushes his teeth,
shaves. Seated on the toilet, pants
pooled around his ankles, hands pressed together,
and forehead bowed in prayer, he asks all
the saints to intercede on his behalf, to free him of
the cramps puckering his innards with spasms dark
as sin. He showers, dresses, and applies his cologne;
a cup of coffee awaits him in the kitchen. He takes
an Omeprazole with his breakfast, sitting ram-
rod straight, head held high with the help
of his tie; if it weren't for the knot,
who knows how far it would roll. The last
time was a disaster: his head was found, drunk
and unkempt, outside a brothel. The news
made all the papers. His driver and bodyguard take
him to work. Along the way, he's distracted
by the blemishes multiplying across
his hands. First Klonopin of the day.
The office receives him, bursting with papers,
trade agreements, bilateral trafficking,
the purchase and sale of bonds, stocks, properties,
red blood cells, leukocytes, platelets, bilirubin,
serotonin, just look at these blood sugar levels,
this spike in cholesterol. It's time to implement
the exchange control. Blood is always wasted.
Ibuprofen for his headache, plus the minutes
of the transatlantic and hematological free
trade agreement. We have to cover up

the raw earth with whatever we can, with whatever
we've got. Order and progress, or just
what's closest. Second Klonopin of the day. And
God set him a task: to name the beasts
that roam the earth, the birds without memory or
ambitions, the fish that will never find
themselves a shadow. The minister obeyed.
He devoted himself to fabricating names in a grainy
voice, and soon the time had come
for bank packages, real estate
bubbles, inflation with its false teeth
and eyes full of lead. The Eucharistic miracle
had been performed: the flesh was tin and wine
petroleum. It wasn't easy, not at all. Third Klonopin
of the day: the austere miracle of the multiplying
fishes and Clonazepam, just as the man from Galilee
effected it when he invented bank interest.
And Diclofenac for his back, please. When
he reaches the bar, the whiskey of the end
times, he's sure that his blood pressure is up, but
there's no Losartan left: a tragedy for the national
economy. It's impossible to predict what will happen to
the gross domestic product if it doesn't settle down, but the music
torments him, he hasn't eaten, and the aluminum of other
people's laughter makes him nervous. Tonight he shows
up at his lover's house, willing to approve the exploitation of
all the natural resources demanded by the country's
development. Its fate hangs on the incandescent
tremor of his heart. After they fuck, he shuts himself
up in the bathroom and takes a piss, humming "Imagine." He's
had it stuck in his head all day.

XXI
NATURAL HISTORY OF DEBRIS: POMPEII

Outside, the usual: shops and newsstands, eight-euro
soda bottles, people fanning away the heat with
tourist brochures. Buses with their din of exasperated
metal and their brakes' long screech. Inside is only
heat and stone, stone determined not to fall asleep,
not to crumble when looked at, stone made of a
pasty faith. Buildings' remnants stretch across the ground
like the account of a long fever, as if passion
could only be horizontal.

But this place isn't empty. Its
cracks and tunnels teem with miniscule life, which has no titles or
monuments. Centipedes, worms, crickets, beetles: an entire
sleepwalking city. I walked through it, treading the houses,
entering uninvited, trying to read the graffiti and the
marks left on the walls, letters like fruit, ruptured
and porous. I looked at the letters and thought
that the angel of history must have the wings of a disoriented insect,
a fly unhinged by the luxuriant fragrance of someone's kitchen, a
cockroach whose wings puff up with a gust that blows
in from nowhere: it flies from here to there, shaken by the current,
dizzy, until it bumps into a window and goes in.

Years later, in Quebec,
I found that someone had written *sox pistols* in a sidewalk's
wet cement. The morning was a clot of solid blue; above
the phrase were a few trapped ants, unable to lift
their feet and free themselves of the substance embracing
them like deafness. *Haec est materia gloria nostrœ*, Pliny
scribbled there somewhere, on the bathroom walls of history, alongside
the phone numbers promising easy sex and a doodle of a masturbating
Caesar.

XXXII
(LULLABY FOR MALENA)

Sleep, my girl, so that all the stray bullets
of the world may sleep with you. May
the earth's bleached bones be soothed
for today, may the brusque sky overhanging
us cease to swing. Your body asks this
peace of you in exchange for enduring
the voracity of your hands, your questions'
weight in hunger—in exchange for your impatient
height in the sun. Sleep for everyone who can't
sleep, counting the drops of cold sweat
the night streaks on the window panes. May
terror slip past you like the merest
murmur, like the body of a mare discerned against
the dark. May your stunned flesh rest
in the sound released by the trees when they fall.
Sleep on the other shore of these words
I lull you with, lighter than your shadow,
words I've only partly taught you and
which serve only to slow down
invisibility. The ones who sow rats' teeth in
the damp earth are far away. May the legs
of your bed be so tall that the ocean never
skims you; may the dogs never come
to chant outside your bedroom door.
May space be true to you, and boundless.
And may all paradises be already lost or
still to lose. I've tucked white roots under your pillow,
fine threads that reach down into the second-
to-last breath of childhood. Sleep your gentle sleepiness:
the soft stone of your laughter rests on your still
forehead. I'll come to wake you soon, when the grain
of morning in your skin has opened.

XXXIII

Here's my passport. Yes, my
visa's valid. I have the papers
to confirm it. The purpose of
my visit? Tourism. No, I'm not
transporting any alcohol or tobacco. No,
I don't have any unpasteurized products,
organic materials, or unsanitary
trinkets. I haven't been to a farm
recently; I can't remember the last time
I did. I don't have a license to
carry firearms. I've never
touched a gun. In my carry-on luggage
there are no bottles over 300 milliliters
in volume. The purpose of my
visit? I travel for the same reasons as
everyone else: out of innocence, or because
I believe what I read in books, that there's
somewhere out there where my name
won't reach me, where I can finally
take it in vain. No, there are no whips,
handcuffs, vibrators, or harnesses
in my luggage. Or documents essential
to some nation's peace. I'm not transporting
animal or vegetable species; I left my carnivorous
plants behind, in childhood. Any organs I carry
are neatly tucked away under my skin,
some prematurely coated in rust
and fat. These pills, you ask?
Circulation can't stay static; I can't
have any baffled blood running through
my veins; my breath can't stall
in my throat like a fist of fog:
it'd shatter my teeth and palate.

The purpose of my visit? Because I'm no
longer myself and my home is no longer
my home. You, sir, with your badges
and your uniform, your anthem and
your pledge of allegiance, you'll never
understand that a country is a handful
of stolen words. And someday they
must be returned. That's exactly what I'm doing
right now: I'm leaving the words wherever
I can, wherever they'll let me, even if
their taste has soured. I'm paying off
a debt with these bleary words, which blink
in the zenith lighting. In the city
where I was born, everyone has their debts and
there's always someone to collect them. There,
miracles are a danger like any other,
a stray bullet, a natural disaster. There, all
skins wake with the same innocent
hangover. The purpose of my visit? Because
in the places where no one speaks my language
the body is a disappearance: there's a
transparency that suddenly gangrenes my
flesh, no syllable can restore me, no one
can see me. But I don't travel without a suitcase.
My city is made of paper. I can fold
it up and stuff it in my pocket;
it's shaped like a notebook, like a knowing
touch. There, the saints brawl,
change water into rum, drive Empire
motorcycles, and sleep off their trifling eternity
in clay statues. In my city, we
carry our dead in our pockets.
You can't leave them at home; they
disappear, they tear off into the beyond or
are stolen for resale—they don't leave
so much as a little pillar of salt in exchange.

It’s not really a city; it’s a slow
fever that eats at the valley, haggard,
furious. The purpose of my visit? I’ve spent
years dreaming of a whale that swallows me up
and shelters me for months behind its plaster
teeth, in its belly’s soft night, before
it finally spits me out on unfamiliar shores.

NOTES

Poem VII is dedicated to the memory of Eugenio Hernández.

Poem VIII is dedicated to Harry Abend.

Poem XI is dedicated to Juan Luis Landaeta.

Poem XII is dedicated to Víctor García Ramírez.

LA CIENCIA DE LAS DESPEDIDAS

I

(PASAJE DE IDA)

Miramos la pantalla de salidas y el
próximo vuelo
y el próximo
y el próximo,
todos despegando con la misma
precisión sorda, como niños obedientes,
temerosos de la mano divina que castiga. El cielo no
los abrazará con la devoción que suponen;
sólo les guarda insomnio, turbulencias,
ansiolíticos para navegar a través de las nubes
sin entrar en pánico.

Filas de gente, maletas, bolsos,
tickets, recuerdos regados como aserrín
por el suelo. Todo
con impaciencia, con un hambre nerviosa
que vacía las cosas desde adentro, regalándoles
el paraíso duro de la espera
y la huida.

Aeropuertos, hospitales, la misma pulcritud
áspera, la misma luz encanecida, como si
toda esa blancura pudiera
eclipsar los cuerpos que van y
vienen, cancelar los fluidos que se excretan,
el sudor blando
que a fin de cuentas es el único testimonio
de nuestro paso por aquí.
Ni un solo órgano hecho
para esta fuga. Apenas el cuerpo recortado,
incómodo de tan nítido, reconociéndose

a duras penas en el número del vuelo, en
la puerta de embarque, el aire flaco con el que
nos atragantamos en el preoperatorio.
(Y a todas estas,
¿quién diseña estas planillas de ingreso, quién escoge
la tipografía de los boletos, su tamaño, quién
les inculca esta inclinación a traspapelarse?)
El cuerpo
nudo de válvulas, materia grasa, tensado por ligamentos.
El cuerpo embrutecido por la cadencia de los motores,
el sonido del tiempo hambreado
que nos rasga vetas en la carne.
Así suena el hambre, como el próximo vuelo.

Entonces miro tus manos, que siempre
están húmedas y le
roban el filo a todo lo que tocan.
Miro su piel asombrada, temerosa mientras
aprietan el pasaje y revisan
que los documentos de
identidad sigan a salvo
en los bolsillos,
estampitas de santos y exvotos por ofrecer

–mientras el techo del aeropuerto
se levanta y echa a volar, dejándonos
calvos bajo el cielo de arena.

II

Odiseo no volvió a Ítaca. Pasó demasiados años
en el mar, masticado por esa mandíbula triste.
Tantos, que hasta los dioses
se cansaron de observarlo y perseguirlo,
quedándose dormidos finalmente. Cuando
regresó, ya no parecía el mismo. No tenía señas
que lo identificaran, no tenía marcas ni
cicatrices. Tampoco llevaba pasaporte
o cédula de identidad. Más bien parecía
un muchacho turco o un flaco chipriota con apenas
algunas canas, la piel tostada de tanto andar
bajo el sol. Alcanzó la playa luego de que su barco
naufragara. La isla no tenía un nombre que él
entendiera: sus montes y bosques ásperos
olían diferente, sus pájaros cantaban dormidos.
Isla lagarto pedregoso bajo el mediodía.
No halló su palacio, ni penélopes hacendosas y oscuras,
ni telémacos barbicortos. No había pretendientes
en las cercanías; acaso alguien ya los había matado.
Encontró solamente un pueblo de pocas calles,
exasperado por la luz y el rechinar de las olas
color estaño. Nadie lo reconoció, ni él
reconoció a nadie. Los perros hacían ruido a su paso,
ladridos como el brillo descoyuntado del bronce.
Confundido, decidió navegar hasta el continente.
Pero la vieja costumbre de la hospitalidad se
había perdido; ya nadie estaba dispuesto
a ofrecer techo a cambio de un relato o
una canción. Lo metieron preso por no llevar
documentos y por expresarse en un lenguaje
ininteligible, viejos huesos que se rompen.
Era como si todo el mundo se hubiera tapado

los oídos con cera de abeja. Trató de explicar
que viajar es perder lenguas, no ganarlas, pero
fue en vano. En la cárcel, no fue capaz de
contar sus recuerdos a nadie, no pudo narrar a los
otros presos sus hazañas: por primera vez
estaba desnudo. Los crímenes que había cometido
durante la guerra se enquistaban en su memoria, dátiles
que al pudrirse despedían un olor quieto y brutal.
Con su conocida maña, logró escapar a los
pocos meses, esta vez sin cegar a nadie.
Se instaló en una zona poco frecuentada
de la ciudad, cerca de los aserraderos. Allí consiguió,
no se sabe cómo, trabajo de carpintero.
Dormía en albergues; sus noches eran gruesas,
inflexibles, lo sofocaban como si estuvieran
hechas con piel de buey. En las
avenidas, perseguía jovencitos de brazos
morenos, a veces con éxito. Hubiera querido
tomarlos a la fuerza, botín reclamado por derecho,
o seducirlos con astucias, pero sabía
que se entregaban por lástima. Luego
pasaba la madrugada sentado al borde de la cama,
gimiendo como quien se sienta en la arena: la
cal de esas pieles se le quedaba en los labios.
Poco después perdió el empleo. Terminó
viviendo de limosnas y pequeños hurtos.
El hambre lo había quebrado, alucinaba ángeles
desnudos como el vidrio o como el ojo de ciertos peces.
Se sabe que no alcanzó la vejez. Algunos
creen que murió de inanición, pero hay quien dice
que recibió un navajazo peleando con otro mendigo.

III
(EL COLOQUIO DE LOS PÁJAROS)

En medio del Palacio de los Nazaríes, una
estancia rectangular, sin techo, cuyo nombre
se me escapa. Piedra mansa que ya
no tiene señorío sobre nadie, con un estanque breve
como ombligo, como ojo único, como
boca en pleno bostezo de agua. Me siento en
las escaleras, aplastado por este calor que
ahueca los huesos y los vuelve flautas, rodeado
de turistas venidos de Asia o Europa del Este,
insolados y frenéticos. Por encima
de nosotros, decenas de vencejos atraviesan
piando el aire estrecho, ensordeciendo las
paredes y el clic de las cámaras y el bullicio,
tapando el verano entero con esa sola voz hecha
de cuchillos, tejas, tinta impalpable, los
tendones del viento, como queriendo impartir
una lección, una revelación a los cuerpos
sudorosos que pasarán aquí la tarde y
volverán a casa, mostrarán las fotos a sus
familiares y les hablarán de un edificio
infestado de pájaros, una lección que
enseña, quizás, que el primer hombre no era
el primer hombre, sino un recorrido apenas, una
vía estriada de sangre y bilis y médula fulgurante
como un atardecer de agosto,
y que el primer pájaro no era el primer
pájaro, sino un sonido amasado hasta el espesor
de la fuga, y que entre uno y otro sólo cabe
la claridad sin cabeza de este día. Pero capaz no
quieren decir nada de esto; capaz se contentan
con volar de grieta en grieta, permaneciendo allá arriba,

donde la eternidad es otro animal por domesticar.
Me quedo sentado mientras pasan vencejos y turistas.
Sus gritos contentos son niños sin bautizar.

IV

(TUBINGA, UN MES CUALQUIERA)

Nunca he estado en Tubinga,
ni he caminado junto a sus aguas y sus
casas. No sabría decir cómo llegar
a la torre donde Hölderlin firmaba
los poemas que Celan escribiría mucho
después, en un alemán que era como
una región desasida del espacio, peleada
con el tiempo, un territorio de encabalgamientos
inesperados, de cesuras y ojos
implacables. Nunca aprendí a hablar alemán,
no tengo el pasaporte que me permitiría
transitar ese país de sílabas encandiladas,
fundado tan sólo por
dos personas, esa nación no declarada, de
contrabando, que multiplica sus sombras
con cada nueva traducción. Si me dejaran
varado en Tubinga, no sabría decir
siquiera el nombre del lugar, no
sabría decir Tübin-
Tübin-
Tübingen.
La palabra me mordería la lengua.
Palabra cocodrilo de ríos imprevistos,
serpiente de los mares que se encharcan
somnolientos, sonoros, bajo el paladar.
Palabra hambrienta de bocas
que la pronuncien. Tü-bin-
gen. Tü-bin-gen. Tü-
se enrosca detrás de los labios, pone
huevos en la oscuridad de la saliva,
en el nido inquieto de la voz. Nunca

he estado en esta palabra, no sabría
decir cómo llegar a ella, ni a la torre,
ni a la tierra que guarda el poema
cuando lo que resta es tiempo de penuria.

V

Las uñas cortadas, los dientes
de leche, los pellejos arrancados
con diligencia, la ropa amnésica, el
sudor, la tinta invisible del cuerpo,
la sílaba abierta de la sangre
menstrual, el semen seco hecho
cicatriz de sal sobre la sábana.
Toda esta crónica ilegible, aceite
que se empoza muy abajo
de los días, que se calienta con
rabia pegostosa. Testamento
amontonado del cuerpo, despojos
y vértebras enclenques y fluidos
a medio cuajar.
Lo que se gasta, pero no
se mide. Lo que nos roban
las ratas mientras dormimos,
las migajas y los grumos como
coágulos breves fermentados
en el sueño. La piel, ese agua delgada
que todos navegan con el mismo miedo.

VI
(HISTORIA NATURAL DEL ESCOMBRO: HUESOS)

Al rato los golpes dejan de doler porque
caen en el mismo lugar, uno y otro, uno
y otro, solamente suenan, pam pam pam
pam, como cuando alguien corta leña en el
bosque, alguien que uno no conoce, alguien
que no le dice su nombre a los árboles antes
de cortarlos. Pam pam pam pam: el puño en
la barriga, hundiéndose con ganas, la correa
contra la espalda, la bofetada a contramano, el
hilo de sangre caminándome sonámbulo
por la frente. A mí y a mis hermanos, casi
todos los días, cada vez que algo le molesta,
cada vez que está de mal humor. A veces saca
el revólver y dispara contra la pared, contra
el techo, para que nos callemos, para que lo
dejemos dormir en paz. Entonces salimos
al porche y jugamos con las herramientas
oxidadas, armamos muñecos con las palas
y los martillos, cazamos ratas con las hoces
porque los conejos son demasiado rápidos
y papá no nos deja probar con su pistola.
Somos ocho, nos arreglamos como podemos,
una vez hasta hicimos un trineo con una
puerta vieja. Papá nos llamó idiotas: aquí
nunca cae nieve. Cuando me aburro voy
al corral que está en el patio trasero y hablo
con los cerdos que tenemos allí. Les cuento
historias, les digo qué quiero ser cuando
crezca, cuando me vaya a vivir a la ciudad.
Papá cree que estoy loco, creo que por eso me
pega más que a mis hermanos. Pam pam pam

pam. Un día se le fue la mano y así terminé aquí. Me caí al piso pero no lo sentí. Dejé de respirar pero no me di cuenta sino al rato; a veces uno pierde costumbres de toda la vida de las maneras más raras. Tenía los ojos cerrados y aún así sabía que papá estaba caminando nervioso a mi alrededor. Poco después me cargó hasta el patio y me echó aquí, en el corral. Al rato los cerdos empezaron a morderme. Quería decirles que pararan, pero la verdad no me dolía. Y bueno, papá casi nunca les da de comer. Cuando ya no quedaba carne, se comieron también los huesos. Dejaron algunos para que pudiera seguir haciéndoles compañía, contándoles historias para que no se aburran en el calor y el lodo. Cuando uno se muere, aprende un montón de palabras nuevas. De pronto conoce cuentos que nunca había escuchado. Son relatos que vienen de lejos, como el pam pam pam pam de los golpes sobre la corteza de la piel, de muy lejos, de lugares donde ni siquiera papá ha estado, de gente que nadie de por aquí ha conocido. Uno también aprende a escuchar mejor cuando está muerto, cuando ya ni siquiera tiene orejas. Así fue como oí cuando papá salió en las noticias de la tele: efectivos del departamento de policía de Kansas City acudieron a finales del mes de noviembre al domicilio de Michael A. Jones, de 44 años de edad; la policía había recibido quejas por parte de los vecinos: disparos sonaban a menudo provenientes de la casa de Jones; al parecer, éste golpeaba a su esposa y a sus hijos, uno de los cuales sigue desaparecido. Al poco tiempo

llegaron varios hombres uniformados y
registraron la casa de arriba a abajo. Tardaron
en revisar el corral. No me gustó que lo hicieran,
molestaron a mis cerdos, que no tenían la culpa
de nada: chillaron cuando desenterraron mis huesos.
¿Quién les iba a contar historias ahora? ¿Quien les
iba a hablar de las cosas que nunca verían? No
se preocupen, les dije, mientras me metían en unas
bolsitas plásticas, sean pacientes, yo vuelvo pronto.

VII
(ISLANDIA)

Me costó años descubrir que la nieve
es la forma menos amorosa del sueño.
Tardé en comprender que
detrás de su blanco sólo hay más blanco,
un hambre plana que nadie ha sabido
dibujar, una mano furtiva que hurta
transeúntes desprevenidos cuando nadie la ve.
Recibí esta nieve como quien recibe las llaves
de una casa que no ha sido construida. Y por
encima de tanta blancura atea, ese
sol sin orgullo, que no cuida de nadie.
Al menos el sol del trópico vela por la sed
que rasga la garganta, regala ese sudor metálico
que nos destiñe el nombre, que presiona
la frente con el peso de una promesa. Aquí
la palabra sol no me recuerda nada. No
lleva un ojo encandilado por dentro, un cielo
pupila cóncava. Se me escurre de la boca, se seca
incómoda en la comisura de los labios. No se arrastra
por el cielo, no me despierta golpeando su martillo claro
contra la campana de mi cráneo. Los techos pálidos,
las calles que se extienden sin saber a dónde,
el santo y seña de los guantes y los abrigos: sigo
sin dominar estas maneras. Camino con
cuidado, a la manera de quien oye voces a
medias y se confunde, creyendo que hablan
su idioma. Conmigo, siempre, este frío
como un pan sin dueño.

VIII
(PEQUEÑA ELEGÍA PARA EL SARGENTO SCHMIDT)

Un reloj de bolsillo, dorado y pasado de moda,
que sonaba como el castañear de dientes minúsculos
si se lo acercaba al oído: esto fue lo único
que quedó intacto en el amasijo de carne y
andamios rotos que era el sargento Schmidt.
Terminaba el año 1944 y la pared de un
edificio lo aplastó en Jarosław, durante los
bombardeos. El derrumbe quebró el tallo
de su espalda, endeble, ciega. Sus órganos
se desprendieron como frutos tiernos. Apenas
en ese momento entendió que la sangre está hecha
de caballos ansiosos por escapar. Ninguno de
sus subordinados tuvo tiempo de recoger
los restos. No hubo morgue ni funerales; le tocó
la fosa común, igual que a tantos otros.
Arriba, las nubes brillaban como huesos.
Pero todo esto es apenas suposición. No
sé si realmente su nombre era Schmidt y su
rango sargento. No sé si pertenecía a la
Wermacht o las SS, si permaneció en Polonia
durante toda la guerra, si tenía hijos, esposa,
amante, si prefería el té o el café, qué pensaba
del traqueteo de las botas militares, el bostezo
de los panzer, el sonido de los techos cuando
se rinden al agotamiento y dejan caer sus espaldas
ancianas, si el olor del cuero le daba náuseas, si
temía a sus superiores, si conocía algún poema
estúpido de memoria, cuántos hermanos tenía,
quién padecía insomnios por su culpa, si alguna
vez descubrió que los muertos van a la
playa por las noches a bailar y beber

una guarapa dulce, cuántas puertas tenía la casa
donde nació, quién le enseñó las palabras que no
se atrevía a usar, o por qué soñaba cada noche
con perros que le lamían las manos.
Lo único que sé es que en 1940, durante la
ocupación de Jarosław, un oficial estaba
encargado de expulsar a los residentes
del número 4, calle Grodzka, hacerlos arrodillarse
en la acera y ejecutarlos. En vez de hacerlo, les
ordenó abandonar la ciudad y huir hacia
la frontera soviética. Tal vez fue la única
ocasión en que manejó la materia aguda, feroz
de la piedad. El país de Nod es pequeño y cabe
en el bolsillo. Su peso no siempre es imperceptible.

IX
(IL MIGLIOR FABBRO)

Es cosa rara, la sombra. Pertenece al cuerpo, brota
de él, pero no está hecha de la misma
materia sorda, sino de su distancia, su falta:
es el cuerpo a contracorriente. Aparece sin
aviso, cuando la luz nos golpea y derriba
algo en nosotros, algo que no hace ruido
al caer, que permanece en el suelo, humillado. Por
eso prefiero salir de noche, cuando el sol
no cuelga sobre la cabeza como un hacha o
un grito al que alguien ha sacado filo, con esa
claridad que lo vuelve transparente a uno y
descubre todos los andamios mal juntados bajo
la piel, la enramada desquiciada de las venas.
Cuando puedo pagarlo, me gusta ir a uno que
otro bar. El Pullman, por ejemplo, allá en la
Solano, sobre todo los martes de música retro. Me
siento en la barra, pido una de tercio y me la
tomo poco a poco, rindiéndola. Casi nunca paso
de tres. Antes íbamos al ZZ o La Fragata y bebíamos
whisky, cuando al salir después de las siete a uno
no le mordía la espalda ese sudor frío, ese sudor perro.
Los amigos se murieron o se fueron del país, son
los garabatos de la memoria, las astillas que
dejo por donde paso; ahora pido cerveza y bebo
solo, porque en esta vaina basta pedir etiqueta
negra para recibir vat69. Llego y busco un
espacio donde los bombillos no puedan
ejercer su estupidez y donde sea fácil
espiar a las parejas. No atraigo la atención
de nadie, quien va a querer escuchar mi voz
arrugada mientras cuento las nimiedades del día,

cómo cada vez escribo menos porque las letras
saltan de la página como pulgas y se esconden
–después paso todo el día rascándome las
picadas, mira. Quién va a querer, ¿ah? Ya no
tengo ganas de robarle el sueño a las palabras.
Así que me siento en el Pullman y me dedico
a amasar el aire. Pero esta noche alguien se me
acercó. Un chamo delgado, moreno, no más
de treinta años. Me tocó el hombro y sonrió,
pidiendo que le invitara algo. Daniel Arnaldo, estás
hecho: le gustaban los tipos mayores, imagino.
Conversamos no sé de qué,
me está costando recordar las cosas. Estoy seguro
de que lo invité a mi apartamento y aceptó. Tengo
claro el tacto de sus manos remedándome la piel,
su cuerpo bajo el mío, hundiéndose en la cama
como un pez que busca fondo. Debo
haberme dormido sobre nuestra saliva cansada.
De esto no tengo duda porque me despertaron
unos ruidos. El muchacho estaba registrando el
cuarto con prisa. Me senté y lo llamé. No le habré
dicho su nombre, porque no lo sabía. Se volteó y
vi que tenía un cuchillo que habrá sacado de
mi cocina. La luz, la puta luz de la mañana se
reflejaba sobre él. Y fue ese brillo que me hundió
callado en el estómago. Creo que no reaccioné, ni
siquiera puse cara de sorpresa, todavía no tenía
el cuerpo de este lado de la vigilia. Me vi la raja,
no parecía algo que pudiera pasarle al cuerpo, una
boca mal formada, una boca a la que le comieron
los labios. Miraba desorientado, esperando que
saliera otra cosa, no ese caldo rabioso que yo
tenía por dentro, sino algo más, expulsado
de su escondite, sin saber dónde meterse.

X

Mi padre tenía dos nacimientos, pero una
sola vida. En todos esos papeles que guardaba
con celo para que dieran testimonio de su
existencia, estaba inscrito un día diferente
al que celebrábamos en su cumpleaños. Con
una de esas fechas mi padre, cansado,
sobornaba a la muerte.

Mi hermana y yo siempre le pedíamos
que nos hablara de su infancia. No
había olvidado casi nada. Conservaba intactos
el caserío, el pueblo, su madre, sus hermanos. Los
animales que vagaban amenazantes entre
los árboles, imprecisos como el sueño de alguien
más. Cada hoja con su linaje, cada fruto
con la ceguera tibia de su pulpa. Cerca
de la casa, el río, el rencor inagotable.

En esa orilla desapareció por primera vez
a los cinco o seis años. Se levantó en la entraña
caliente de la madrugada y salió sin ser
notado. La casa estaba aplacada, apenas
debían oírse sus pasos sobre las ramas delgadas,
huesos astillados. Caminaba dormido, tenía los
párpados sellados con cera y polvo. Cuenta que
lo atraparon junto a la corriente, a punto
de lanzarse, buscando esos peces que son
como hilos que alguien trenzó para la huida.

En sus historias, todas las cosas tenían un
gesto equívoco; daba la impresión de que
estaban disfrazadas de sí mismas. Las cubría

una corteza dulce, donde con los años había crecido
el musgo y donde las hormigas abrían caminos
sin ser vistas. Su propio padre apenas se dejaba
recordar. Los rasgos se le habían extraviado, capaz
los había perdido en una apuesta mal habida, no era
un hombre, era más una presencia cuya densidad
y volumen no se podían medir bien, una cólera, unos
nudillos, el deseo acéfalo y brutal. Colgaba inerte
en el centro de la memoria de mi padre, como
aquel toro que vio una vez, de niño, guindando boca
abajo, ojos en blanco, garganta abierta, mientras
la arcilla suave de su sangre se vertía en una olla.

Me solían decir que tengo las manos de mi padre.
No sé si también tenga las del suyo. Pero quizás
ellos tienen las mías, puede que sea yo quien
se las haya prestado, puede que ahora con cada ademán
y cada pliegue les esté dejando marcas.
Hay que leer la herencia al revés, recorrerla
con los dedos como quien sigue la puntuación
desigual del Braille. Navegar hacia arriba: hacer
entonces un barco con la madera triste del cuerpo.

XI
(CURSO INTENSIVO DE BIOPOLÍTICA 2)

Reportan los principales periódicos que hoy
un grupo de empresarios, en colaboración con
la Alcaldía Mayor de Caracas, acaba
de fundar una compañía que ofrece, por un módico
precio, la posibilidad de hondos recorridos a través
de la ciudad. Emigrados nostálgicos y extranjeros
curiosos podrán investigar las zonas agrestes de la urbe
y entrar en contacto con sus habitantes nativos
en una camioneta blindada conducida
por un profesional armado. El vehículo estará
abastecido con alimentos y bebidas de
primera calidad, así como productos
de las empresas patrocinantes. Tras firmar una
serie de autorizaciones, los exploradores podrán
participar de excursiones para buscar el origen
del Guaire, nuestro Ganges, y fotografiar la fauna
exótica que se apuesta en las terrazas de los
edificios u observa desde las ventanas
con ojos como charcos de agua
tiesa. Varios políticos prominentes, tanto
de izquierda como de derecha, han reservado ya
sus pasajes. El folleto promete a los expedicionarios,
en un tono más bien lírico, que el trayecto les
"descubrirá los mecanismos leves, casi
tiernos, de la misericordia." Inmediatamente
después aconseja a los participantes que
no saquen las manos del vehículo durante
el recorrido, ni den de comer a los
caraqueños, pues sus cuerpos ya no están
adaptados a ciertos productos. También
se les pide guardar silencio o hablar

en voz baja, pues el aislamiento ha convencido
a los habitantes de la ciudad de que su lengua
es la única hablada en el mundo –y una cadena
de ruidos insólitos podría ahuyentarlos. Además,
añade el documento, así podrán escuchar
“el susurro que intercambian los venezolanos
cuando creen que nadie los observa, un sonido
desvencijado, como un billete viejo que pasaran de
mano en mano.” Numerosas celebridades han manifestado
frente a las cámaras su interés por conocer estos parajes
insólitos, cubiertos por un sol que es una gota de aceite.

XII
(LEIBNIZ, MON AMOUR)

En alguno de los mundos posibles, los árboles
pesan menos que la suma de todas sus hojas,
el tiempo se mide en parpadeos y la gente
pasa largos ratos cada noche deshilvanando
la luz para que amanezca. La antropofagia
se ha vuelto la única forma aceptable del amor.
Pero solamente en el mejor de los mundos
posibles hay quienes pasan las madrugadas
en vela buscando el modo de hacer la pena de
muerte más eficaz, menos engorrosa para los vivos.
Hasta han escrito una lista con sus objeciones:

1. La silla eléctrica gasta demasiada energía. Los
edificios cerca de la cárcel se quedan sin luz
durante las ejecuciones. La gente de los alrededores
se queja del humo y el olor a carne quemada.

2. El fusilamiento despierta a los vecinos. Algunos
incluso se han asomado a sus ventanas, pistola
en mano, para responder al fuego.

3. La guillotina requiere cloro, desinfectantes,
trabajo de conserjería. No hay presupuesto para
contratar tal cantidad de personal.

4. El verdugo casi nunca encuentra la vena
al primer intento. La inyección letal tarda
demasiado en hacer efecto: el condenado padece
durante horas, creando toda clase de problemas
de marketing y recursos humanos. Además, las drogas
desaparecen misteriosamente del depósito.

En este mundo se saben torpes: por eso muchos
demandan el chasquido tranquilizador
de la tráquea que se quiebra en la horca: rostro
deformado por la hinchazón, lengua colgando, gruesa.
Sepultan a los ejecutados con piedras en la garganta
para que no protesten. Duermen relajados porque no
comprenden bien el modo en que comercia la muerte,
qué pide a cambio de sus servicios, cómo no se
deja domesticar ni dice a nadie cómo se llama –porque
no puede, porque su nombre es una sucesión continua e
indefinida de puntos estirada sobre un plano, nada más.

XIII

Viajamos: es el espacio que nos deletrea.
Si hubiera un dios que velara por nosotros, un
dios para los tránsitos, las bifurcaciones,
las desviaciones, debería ser entonces un dios
minúsculo. Mientras miro por la ventana
del tren cómo se escapan los edificios, niños
que corren asustados, imagino ese dios cuyo
nombre sería un misterio porque inadvertidamente
lo habría dejado en el asiento de un avión.
No tendría ritos ni templo, no ofrecería consuelos
ni pruebas, no elegiría tribu alguna. Nadie le
daría una palabra en maitines o completas, sus
oraciones serían las madrugadas en blanco
pasadas en estaciones de autobús o en aeropuertos,
con la respiración enlodada porque a esa hora
llueve en los bronquios. No conversaría con otros
dioses que, de todos modos, tampoco existen.
Apenas diría su canción a quien con él fuera.
No castigaría el robo o el adulterio: sabría
que todo camino es un robo y toda palabra
un adulterio. Tendría demasiados hijos como para
escoger a uno que lavara nuestros pecados; en
cambio, nos forzaría a migrar, como si se pudiera
absolver la distancia de su vastedad, de su miedo.
Andaríamos tanto, que ya sólo se nos podría
reconocer desde lejos. Su única función consistiría
en encargarse de que los relojes siguieran trabajando,
para que las partidas ocurran, para que no
se filtrara aquí la eternidad. Sería el dios de los
vuelos retrasados, las taquillas cerradas, el olor
a orina y semen dormido de los baños públicos.
Haría de mí apenas cuerpo entre los cuerpos, ya sin

el suplicio de la abstracción. Cambiaría mis ojos
por carbones amargos, volvería mis manos animales
remotos. Me reduciría a la certeza geométrica
y voraz del movimiento. Me mostraría que la
vigilia no es un estado, sino una tarea de destrucción.

XIV
(STRANGE FRUIT)

Los peces no hablan: es bien sabido. Atraviesan
callados el cielo invertido del mar, sus
pendidos como pensamientos ajenos, colgando sobre
la noche boquiabierta. Se dice que no cantan porque temen
que la voz escape, se deslice hasta la superficie,
donde se quedaría flotando, durmiendo el sueño de
las algas. Cuenta Pierre de Vaisière que en junio de 1724
un barco esclavista atravesaba esas voces morosas
camino a Santo Domingo. Llevaba en bodega alimentos en
conserva, agua dulce, ratas y gatos para comerse a las ratas,
y una mercancía humana que sumaba los trescientos. Olía a tedio
y disentería, a cuerpos amontonados, lamidos por el salitre. A
medio recorrido, el capitán empezó a sospechar que dos
esclavos, un hombre y una mujer, planeaban un motín. Para
curarse en salud, decidió hacer de ellos un ejemplo. Frente
a todo el barco, hizo que a ella le pelaran los miembros
a cuchilladas – murió con los huesos enronquecidos de
tanto gritar. A él, después de tajearle el cuello, ordenó arrancarle
el corazón, el hígado, las vísceras para que fueran picados
en exactamente doscientos noventa y ocho pedazos. Abierto, expuesto,
sus brazos y piernas guindaban, moviéndose con el vaivén
del barco. Podía verse el árbol tembloroso que llevaba por
dentro, allí donde el cielo hundía sus raíces rojas.
Cada esclavo recibió uno de los trozos, carne
de su carne perdida. Cerraban la boca como
el mar se cerraba alrededor del barco, boca sin
garganta, sin labios ni encías. Los cuerpos fueron tirados
por la borda. Los recibieron los peces que, en realidad,
no hablan porque son sordos. Los vieron caer y no
se atrevieron a interrogar los ojos en blanco, las hilachas
de piel, las entrañas súbitamente libres. No preguntaron
sus nombres y, por eso, tampoco los sabemos nosotros.

XV
(HISTORIA NATURAL DEL ESCOMBRO: CABEZAS)

La cabeza de Juan el Bautista esculpida por Rodin
en 1887 besa el plato sobre el que descansa, como si
fuera un espejo o una ventana desde la cual se ve
el otro lado de la vigilia. De sus labios no cuelga
una sola bendición más: está cansado de hablar.
Ahora escoge sus palabras con cuidado, pero
necesita que alguien las extraiga de su boca, donde
están escondidas aguantando la respiración. En
su cabello blanco, veteado, se adivina el mar.

*

Frederick Wilhelm Murnau nació en 1888 y murió en
1931. A finales del año 2015 su cuerpo fue exhumado y
su cráneo removido en un cementerio ubicado cerca
de Berlín. Las autoridades creen que los ladrones mutilaron
el cadáver con el propósito de realizar algún ritual. Pero
ese rostro descarnado sólo puede hablarles del sonido
minúsculo que hacen los gusanos al devorar la carne,
cuando realizan su antigua tarea sacramental. Y del
silencio que se hace luego, la arena alojada en las
cuencas vacías y las fisuras, cada grano un punto de
noche sin domesticar. El tedio es lo único que se parece
a la eternidad: hace su trabajo con genuino amor por el detalle.

*

Contrario a lo que cuentan las historias, cuando
despedazaron su cuerpo y dispersaron sus miembros,
no lanzaron su cabeza al río. Decidieron conservarla
en un altar rudimentario: ahí estuvo por años,

pálida e hinchada, ojos en blanco, sangre endurecida
y oscura donde hubiera debido empezar la garganta.
Gente iba a verla desde lugares lejanos para hacerle
preguntas; esperaban que profetizara o cantara, que
ofreciera acertijos como monedas de un país
que nadie ha visto. Casi borrosa, la cabeza de
Orfeo no entona canciones, pero no por eso deja
de entregar algún prodigio: de la comisura de sus
labios brota, día y noche, un hilo de baba tenaz.

XVI

El ruido de los aviones al pasar golpea
la frente del edificio. Estoy sentado viendo
a Bugs Bunny convencer a un cazador de que
no es un conejo. El aire es pálido a las nueve
de la mañana, fino como una hostia. Mis cuatro
años caben con todo su peso en el mueble
que está frente a la TV. Cuando los aviones
atraviesan el cielo, rayándolo, todo se sacude
contagiado por el mismo temblor, como si
de pronto las cosas hubieran decidido exponer
sus entrañas. La geografía de lo cotidiano había
sido sumisa, sin aparecidos ni prodigios;
nadie nos prestaba sus milagros y no teníamos lo
suficiente para pagar uno. Pero esa mañana unos
aviones demolieron la barrera del sonido justo
sobre mi cabeza, sobre mi pelo enmarañado
y somnoliento. La mandíbula del cielo se
dislocaba y dejaba caer un llamado áspero, una
sola palabra toda hecha de piedras. Ya no había
nada en la pantalla, sólo unas barras de colores
y un pitido insistente que parecía querer perforarme
el oído. Corrí a la ventana para ver qué pasaba y mi
padre me hizo agacharme bajo el marco. Entonces
escuché los tiros: uno, dos, tres, precisos. No estoy
seguro de la bala que nos partió aquella ventana
del apartamento en Quinta Crespo: puede que
la haya inventado. Pero ese vidrio roto fue
la capa inaugural de lo que algún día sería mi piel.
Apenas tengo esta escena; el relato vendría
más tarde. Es el mal fotomontaje de la infancia, arritmia
de imágenes deslucidas por el uso, borrosas porque
en la memoria llueve todo el tiempo. El agua

rasca la superficie de las fotos como si
quisiera filtrarse en ellas. Encharcarlas. Inundarlas.

XVII

Estudié la ciencia de la despedida
en los calvos lamentos de la noche.
Osip Mandelstam

En Nataruk, al norte de Kenia, arqueólogos
hallaron los restos de 27 seres humanos
amontonados en la palma seca de lo que
solía ser un lago. La datación por radiocarbono
de conchas y sedimentos minerales permitió
estimar que los cadáveres tenían entre 9.500
y 10.500 años de antigüedad. Se trataba de
un grupo diverso: hombres y mujeres adultos
–una de ellas embarazada–, ancianos, niños.
Varios tenían las manos atadas. Todos
presentaban traumatismos graves, señales
de golpes realizados con objetos
contundentes, como mazos, así como
heridas producto de armas punzopenetrantes.
Los expertos creen que los 27 sujetos fueron
reducidos, ejecutados sistemáticamente y
lanzados al lago, donde el limo se ocupó
de conservarlos. Es así como los cuerpos
aprenden a hablar, a decir la vida sin
elocuencia, en kilos de carne, bilis,
flema y saliva, polvo y brillo inclemente.
La vida labios abiertos, dientes cariados,
osamenta de plomo. Cuero extendido
bajo la furia del mediodía, su ojo tosco y
cóncavo. Desaparición, despedida,
miembro fantasma, ciencia trunca.

XVIII
(DUBIA ET SPURIA)

Fr. 54

Muchos años después, frente al pelotón
de fusilamiento, había de recordar aquella tarde
remota en que su padre, botando espuma por
la boca, se peleó con un hombre en el bar
del pueblo, lo sacó a la callé y lo molió a golpes.
Los pequeños dientes enrojecidos
brillaban en el suelo, rodaban como hormigas aterradas.

*

Fr. A 3

Cada noche, Perséfone compra un ticket
en la estación de Frankin Avenue / Botanic Garden y
pasa horas recorriendo el metro. Uno de sus ojos
solamente puede ver lo que ya ha sido; el otro la traiciona
y le hace ver lo que nunca podrá ser. Aún no ha descubierto
si se trata del izquierdo o el derecho. Viaja esperando
a que un extraño se le acerque y le ofrezca una granada.

*

Fr. D 7

Un día, las tropas de ocupación desaparecieron.
No pasaron aviones o helicópteros, no se oyó
el ruido de los camiones al partir. El campamento
estaba intacto: armas, municiones, vehículos uniformes,
provisiones, todo guardado con algo parecido

al pudor. Meses luego descubrimos que
habían encontrado la manera de cumplir su misión:
bajo los sembradíos y haciendas, alimentando la
tierra, los árboles, los pastos, aquellos soldados se
pudrían rabiosamente. Era demasiado tarde.

*

Fr. 27

Muchos años después, frente al pelotón de fusilamiento,
había de recordar aquella tarde remota en que su padre
lo llevó al prostíbulo. Las chicas lo saludaban de lejos,
dos de ellas aún conservaban los moretones que les había
dejado. En el pueblo no había hielo para reducir la hinchazón.
Se dejó conducir, aún niño, pero no pudo acostarse con
ninguna. El deseo era una rasgadura que supuraba, que le
llenaba la garganta con un líquido desconocido. Estaba mudo,
inmóvil. El ridículo y el escarnio lo aguardaban en casa.

*

Fr. E 9

[...] insepulto, sometido a la lujuria de los buitres.

*

Fr. C 31

Todos lanzaron vítores cuando la cabeza del rey
rodó por el suelo, despegada de su cuerpo por la
nítida pasión de la guillotina. Tras un par de semanas,
sin embargo, empezó a correr un rumor: el rey
conservaba una segunda cabeza oculta en algún lugar.

Se decía que estaba en palacio; otros especulaban
que se hallaba escondida entre las reliquias parlantes
de la catedral. Pero algo parecía irrefutable: desde allí,
todos insistían, aún gobernaba el reino.

*

Fr. A 14

Caronte fuma sentado en la orilla de acá
del río. A su alrededor se agolpan
los muertos, parados porque ya no recuerdan
cómo sentarse. El barquero se
niega a transportarlos, no acepta como
pago por sus servicios chapas de
botellas ni latas de cerveza vacías.

*

Fr. 32

Muchos años después, frente al
pelotón de fusilamiento, había de
recordar aquella tarde remota en que
su padre lo llevó a cazar venados por
primera vez. Disparaba bien a pesar de la
herida que tenía en la mano izquierda –dicen
que había nacido con seis dedos en ella, pero
un buen día agarró un cuchillo y se tajeó
el dedo sobrante. Le enseñó cómo
desollar apropiadamente, cómo extraer las
vísceras y conservar la sangre. Guardaba
para sí los ojos del venado. Era
imposible saber qué hacía con ellos.

*

Fr. A 33

La noche en que murió el presidente, ni una
sola persona se dio cuenta. Los demás habitantes
de palacio bebían, veían porno o simplemente
dormían. Fue al día siguiente que encontraron
su cuerpo ya hinchado, como si se tratara de una
esponja que hubiera guardado dentro de sí
lo que quedaba de la madrugada. Luego de
los gritos y los llantos de rigor, las oraciones
adecuadas, le cerraron los ojos. Pero estos
volvieron a abrirse de inmediato. Sus familiares
y allegados no se acobardaron: los cerraron una
ves más. Y al instante siguiente estaban
de nuevo abiertos. Así pasaron la primera
mitad del día, en esa batalla desigual con los
magnos párpados. Llamaron a ministros, edecanes,
representantes de la cámara de empresarios y hasta
al alto mando militar –nadie supo qué hacer.
No podían enterrarlo así. Finalmente,
el vicepresidente tuvo una idea: sugirió sustituir
ojos y párpados por otros, falsos. Así se hizo.

*

Fr. 15

Muchos años después, frente
al pelotón de fusilamiento, había
de recordar aquella tarde remota
en que su padre le mostró la novela
que había estado escribiendo
durante años, un libro para retener
la suma de los olvidos.

*

Fr. C 5

Vivir la vida de tal manera que quede
intacta cuando la abandonemos,
para que alguien más pueda recogerla del suelo,
estirarla, sacudirle el polvo, vestirla con
holgura. Beber nuestra agua, bostezar
nuestros aburrimientos, reír nuestras ironías
de segunda. Para la vida, continuidad y
plagio son una misma cosa.

*

Fr. E 2

[...] de todos los oficios aprendidos,
sólo [...] desnudez.

*

Fr. 11

Muchos años después, frente al pelotón de fusilamiento, había
de recordar aquella tarde remota en que su padre agonizaba en
la cama, hinchado y denso. Retenía líquido como hacía todo
lo demás, con la misma ira, no quería que restara una sola gota
en el mundo. Deliraba, creía que en pocos días la sed
derrumbaría las casas del pueblo, enloquecería los caballos,
devoraría por dentro a las reses. No había quien lo atendiera, nadie
lo aguantaba. Le habían retirado la jefatura civil y sus otros
hijos vivían en la capital, escapados. Esa noche, tras de mover
el cadáver, encontraron bajo la cama dos bolsas viejas,
como de basura, repletas de huesos de pollo, fotografías
decoloradas, balas y una botella de aguardiente sin abrir.

XIX
(HISTORIA NATURAL DEL ESCOMBRO: RIÑONES)

Nombre del paciente: Adalber Salas Hernández.
Cédula de identidad: ██ ███ ███
Edad: 21 años.
Peso: 63,5 kg.
Talla: 173 cm.
Referido por la doctora ████ █████
El paciente presenta dolor lumbar de fuerte intensidad en el costado derecho, irradiado al epigastrio, tórax y espalda (hombro), actualmente de 15 días de evolución, haciéndose más intenso con la inhalación profunda. Acudió a la emergencia de la clínica, donde detectaron VSG: 52 mm, proteína en orina de 2+, cilindros granulosos (0-4xc) y urocultivos que fueron negativos, con proteinuria de 2,93 g/24h. A los pocos días presentó una induración con limitación de función en la vena del dorso del codo derecho, con discreto edema sin eritema.

[Agujas delineando el espacio entre las
costillas, la extensión opaca de esa región
donde no hay casas, donde no pace ganado,
donde ningún árbol estira el frío de sus
ramas. Agujas trabajando las costillas
como haciendo un grabado, su curva
abrazando el limo fértil de los pulmones.]

Antecedentes personales:
Asma en la infancia.
Niega alergias a medicamentos.
Extracción de 3 cordales el 21 de mayo del 2009. Recibió ibuprofeno cada 12 horas, más diclofenac cada 6 horas y clindamicina cada 10 horas.
Resección de los cornetes nasales y corrección de desviación del tabique.
Episodio febril intenso en noviembre.
Vacunado contra la hepatitis.

[Musgo creciendo en las paredes carnosas,
en los túneles, mordiendo el andamiaje
de la respiración. Algas en
el charco leve de la pleura, trepando
con tenacidad. La tos
un perro con hambre, ladrando,
mordiendo los bronquios.]

Antecedentes familiares:
Padre: vivo, 55 años, laberintitis.
Madre: viva, 51 años, dislipidemia, osteoporosis.
Hermanos: 1H APS.
Historia familiar de diabetes.
HBP: tabáquicos consumo previo, niega actualmente, cafeicos tres tazas diarias, alcohólicos cada 3 días aprox. Medicamentos: marihuana, hachís.
Resto del examen físico no revela alteraciones.

[Órganos artefactos comidos por el uso,
labrados por el desgaste, colgando.
Entre ellos, el lenguaje
tautológico de la sangre, venas que
se estiran para medir distancias
que no sospechamos.
Se va formando una capa de yeso
sobre ellos, poco a poco.

Órganos que penden de su mínimo
insomnio, que no duermen ni dejan dormir.]

Diagnóstico:
Síndrome nefrótico.
Glomerulonefritis membranosa (estadio I-II).
Se requiere descartar la eventualidad de glomerulonefritis membranosa secundaria, por ello se refiere al paciente para evaluación de endoscopia digestiva superior e inferior. Así mismo, se le refiere para realización de

biopsia renal percutánea.

[Órganos como peces que nadan
en un agua ciega. Criaturas sin
testigos, viviendo lejos del
imperio rabioso de la mirada.
Temen descubrir la costa de este
mar subterráneo, orilla desnuda
y encandilada, cuchillo cenital.
Más allá de la piel, la luz:
la forma más acabada del miedo.]

Tratamiento:
Losartán potásico: 50 mg al día.
Omega 3: dos cápsulas al día.
Prednisona: 30 mg a las 8 a.m. y 30 mg a las 4 p.m.
Micofenolato mofetilo: 1 gr cada 12 horas.
Warfarina: 5 mg al día.
Omeprazol: 40 mg al día.
El tratamiento se ajustará según los resultados de los controles mensuales.

[Silencio coral del cuerpo.]

En horas de la mañana del pasado
domingo, el personal entero de la morgue de Colinas
de Bello Monte abandonó súbitamente las
instalaciones de dicha institución, según informa
la Dirección Nacional de Ciencias Forenses.
Testigos afirman que algunos de los empleados
gritaban o corrían sin dirección clara. Poco
más tarde, ese mismo día, se apersonaron frente
al edificio funcionarios del CICPC, acompañados
por diversos expertos y profesores ilustres de la
Escuela de Medicina de la Universidad Central de
Venezuela, junto a un coronel de la Guardia Nacional,
dos médiums, un cura joven y otro viejo, cinco
babalaos. Tras pasar un rato dentro de la morgue,
atravesaron las puertas a duras penas y declararon ante
este y otros medios de comunicación: durante la
madrugada, los difuntos recientemente ingresados a
la institución habían retornado a la vida y
deseaban hacer valer su calidad de ciudadanos
de la República. Ese mismo día y los inmediatamente
posteriores, acontecimientos similares tuvieron
lugar en todos los cementerios e instalaciones forenses
del país. Los muertos, ojerosos y dóciles, se han
congregado poco a poco desde entonces. Sin escatimar
esfuerzos o recursos, han conseguido conformar una
organización sin fines de lucro, la Agencia para la
Protección y el Desarrollo de los Cuerpos en
Descomposición, la APRODECUD. A través de una
campaña de manifestaciones pacíficas y marchas,
pretenden lograr el reconocimiento oficial de sus
derechos civiles y el establecimiento de un escaño
permanente para ellos en la Asamblea Nacional.

El Ejecutivo se ha pronunciado favorablemente, ordenando a toda prisa la creación del Ministerio del Poder Popular para las Relaciones Póstumas. La Iglesia, además de revocar un par de bulas papales, ha guardado silencio. Diversos cultos religiosos han declarado el fin de los tiempos, pero los difuntos mismos parecen un tanto aburridos por la idea. Algunos politólogos eminentes han voceado sus preocupaciones a través de la prensa: cómo puede tener derechos un cuerpo cuya lengua se ha podrido, cuyo pecho está mordido por gusanos mudos. Aunque apenas ha transcurrido una semana desde que iniciaron los sucesos, la APRODECUD ha emitido un comunicado en el que informa a la población nacional –con pulso– que los muertos se niegan a cerrar los ojos, a ser inscritos en el libro de las desapariciones. Empezando con la frase "¡Difuntos del mundo, uníos!", dicho documento insta a los vivos a reconocer su valía como miembros de la patria y a admitirlos como elementos valiosos –"vitales", se lee– para la comunidad. Se refiere con detalle al más allá, lo describe como un lugar empobrecido, sobrepoblado, un mal destino turístico donde las almas en pena se ven obligadas a realizar largas colas para conseguir los bienes más elementales. Dada la exorbitante devaluación de la eternidad, resulta casi imposible comprar nada con la moneda del reino, los dientes que cada quien lleva consigo desde el momento de su muerte. De igual modo, el comunicado enumera una serie de exigencias que la comunidad de difuntos plantea a los habitantes del más acá; entre ellas se destacan la censura de las películas de zombis, por considerarlas injustamente discriminatorias

y promotoras del odio, así como un cambio
en la ortografía de la lengua española:
la introducción de dos nuevas tildes en la
palabra *cadáver*, de manera que se escriba
cádávér, con tres tajos precisos o tres
heridas de bala, pues consideran que así
la palabra representará con mayor justicia
a la colectividad. En una rueda de prensa
dada con motivo del comunicado, el director
de la APRODECUD ha insinuado que uno
de ellos podría postularse como candidato para
las próximas elecciones presidenciales. Expertos
aseguran que, según las últimas encuestas, pronto
el país podría hallarse gobernado por un muerto.

XXI

Los ruidos vuelven cada madrugada, más o menos
a las tres, tres y media. Chasquidos leves, rasguños, sonido
de mínimos huesos que se rompen. Las ratas
conversan detrás de la pared. Nunca
las veo, solamente las oigo andar y trabajar
en la oscuridad intravenosa que media
entre mi apartamento y el del vecino. Las
adivino yendo de un lado a otro, frenéticas,
recorriendo esa geografía provisional, construyendo
pasillos, túneles, depósitos, una ciudad tubular,
un sistema circulatorio para la noche. Y, todo
el rato, ese idioma. Las ratas tienen una lengua
hecha con trozos de plástico y aserrín, de grumos
y palabras que nos han ido hurtando durante siglos,
que no hemos vuelto a pronunciar desde entonces.
Palabras de todas las lenguas habladas alguna vez.
Por eso no importa dónde estemos, los chillidos
de las ratas suenan a recuerdos de infancia.

Las artesanas de la caducidad
están solas. Nadie se ha tomado la molestia de
sermonearles o convertirlas a esta o aquella fe. No
sabemos si creen en la existencia del alma y si acaso
nos consideran merecedores de una. Sabemos, eso sí, que
entierran a sus muertos bajo nuestros colchones.

No permiten que las vea. Sin embargo, cada
mañana encuentro señales en los rincones, testimonios
en forma de heces puntuales, alargadas como una
caligrafía. Puede que sean fragmentos autobiográficos
de alguna de ellas, o la historia anónima
de toda la comunidad, un relato que se estire desde la

creación del mundo hasta el fin de los tiempos, hasta
la última cocina sucia, el último bote de basura. O
quizás estos montoncitos de mierda tan
cuidadosamente alineados sean el lamento
de una rata desesperada porque la carne
es triste y ya ha leído todos los libros.

Cuando duermo, sueño que una de ellas, siempre
la misma, se monta sobre la cama y trota hasta
mi pecho. El torso está abierto: la rata acerca
sus ojos, sus dientes nerviosos, a mis pulmones. Los
examina con cuidado, los huele y
se va, arrastrando la cola desnuda entre
las sábanas. Allí los deja, expuestos, inflados,
dos sacos llenos de aire y espera tibia.

XXII

La lengua que hablo está hecha de preguntas
defectuosas, de frases truncas, recurrentes.
Cada día tocan la puerta pidiendo algo
de comer, amenazando con romperme los dientes.
No sabe bien de dónde proviene; tampoco
le interesa: lengua materna, lengua paterna,
todo es lo mismo para ella.

Entra con sus muletas y llena de tierra la casa.
No tiene modales en la mesa, no sonríe
mientras escucha cómo me quejo. Mi lengua
no tiene piedad conmigo. Me visita porque
está agotada, porque necesita un plato y una cama.
Viene, se echa y me ignora; se hace amiga de los
ratones, las hormigas, las cucarachas que se
esconden en los rincones, bajo los muebles. Recoge
sus historias, las dibuja en el polvo con su dedo
flaco, junto a las macetas llenas de cigarros
a medio fumar.

Mi lengua no tiene sacramentos
ni milagros. Cree que los necesita para
cubrir su desnudez, pero no es cierto. Cree
también que para orar basta con palparse, con
sentir el propio peso halándonos
hacia el centro dormido de la tierra.

Está obsesionada con la exactitud escandalosa
del hambre, cómo nos va deshaciendo poco
a poco, cómo nos va buscando los huesos.
Quisiera despojarse de sí, ser grafiti o valla
publicitaria o garabato sobre el cemento

fresco. Quisiera maldecir y blasfemar con
propiedad, pero eso tampoco le ha sido dado.

Mi lengua nunca ha sabido parecerse
a sí misma. Está hecha de palabras que
se despiden apenas llegan. En ella,
todas las figuras son cuerpos encandilados,
todas las cosas se encorvan como si la luz
quisiera estrujarlas. Habla con impaciencia
y se me queda mirando: en ese momento somos
los dos habitantes de un continente rodeado
por aguas que no duermen.

XXIII
(HISTORIA NATURAL DEL ESCOMBRO: LÁZARO)

Primero fue el aliento cayendo furioso
sobre las aguas. Unas pocas palabras oídas
a medias, piedras estridentes lanzadas
contra la ventana del sueño. Desde niño le
costaba despertar. Contra todos los fueros de la muerte,
manos extrañas toman por los hombros a Lázaro y
lo arrastran al mediodía abrupto como un
acantilado, abren su boca y a la fuerza empujan
en ella la respiración amarga, golpean su pecho
hasta que el corazón arranca, los desagües
del cuerpo se llenan otra vez con el
torrente olvidadizo y sanguinolento, aceite
de motor y diesel. Sale del sepulcro tropezando,
encandilado; la mortaja se le ha caído y los
testigos del milagro pueden ver su carne
oscurecida por la podredumbre, estriada de gusanos,
el mapa de otro mundo. El hedor es insoportable.
Todos se cubren la nariz, algunos vomitan. Lázaro
parpadea bajo el brillo contumaz, le arde
la mirada reseca, no puede enfocarla. Nadie entiende
para qué ha sido traído de vuelta, pero
los periódicos están encantados con la historia. Ya
hay planes para un documental y un reality
show (Lázaro con seis jóvenes en una casa,
aprendiendo a surfear o cocinando frente a una audiencia).
Su foto está por todo Twitter, #levántateyanda. Los
astrólogos no se ponen de acuerdo para elaborar
la carta astral de alguien que ha nacido dos veces.
Él sigue parpadeando. Gesticula, balbucea, las sílabas
se le caen, juguetes torpes. Gemidos, gruñidos. Cómo
encender de nuevo la máquina suave de la voz.

Al poco rato, los testigos se dispersan. Lázaro se
queda solo, aún sin atinar a cubrir su desnudez,
empezando a entender que dios es un músculo ciego.
Finalmente miró al soslayo, se fue y no hubo nada.

XXIV

Guantes semitransparentes, pegajosos, bisturí ya
sin filo, mascarilla, bata blanca demasiado
holgada. Tengo quince años y estoy en el laboratorio,
clase de biología, rodeado de pequeños animales en
jarras de formol, modelos anatómicos hechos
de plástico e instrumentos de precisión que nadie
ha llegado a utilizar. Cada semana, un esqueleto colgante
nos mira desde su esquina, mientras nos esforzamos
por comprender el secreto torpe y viscoso que guardan
los cuerpos vivientes. Hoy tocó traer un corazón
de res. Cargué toda la mañana con su peso negro,
grasiento, encerrado en una hielera para que
no se pudriera. Lo he llevado a cuestas, paciente.
Ahora está en la mesa, sobre una tabla
de disección. No se estremece cuando lo abro,
atravesando el tejido adiposo lo mejor que puedo,
aguantando el olor denso que se pega a la garganta.
Fibras elásticas, membranas, atrios y ventrículos,
todo resistente al tacto, sitios donde crecía
una flora áspera, tierra ansiosa y fría que no
es patria de nadie. Por allí pasaba la sangre llevando
sus pertenencias, su contrabando de cemento, a través
de la válvula pulmonar, para luego pasar por
la aórtica, que se estiraba en un mugido espeso.
Un instrumento enorme, atroz, carne
y grasa terca apretadas con furia, pliegue
sobre pliegue justo como el mío, oculto en
la oscuridad amniótica del pecho, entre los resortes,
engranajes y cables gastados de la caja torácica,
lejos del borde amargo de las cosas, pulsando
como una de esas galaxias hundidas en la distancia,
cuya luz se erosiona y envejece

antes de alcanzarnos. La única virtud de este
aparato fue su ceguera; aquí, en el purgatorio de la
mesa, entre el cuerpo del que fue arrancado y
el paraíso mudo de las lámparas halógenas,
se encuentra expuesto, disminuido, ofreciendo
a la vista los pasajes por los que corría la voz
inarticulada que nos amamantó a todos
alguna vez, la misma que nos dio de comer
el limo ronco de la vida. Está quieto, sin retórica,
puro andamio, lugar de paso. Supo que la distancia no
se mide en metros, sino en desapariciones. Que yo
no es otro; que yo es ninguno, una serie de latidos
amontonados, ruido y óxido, prosodia sin dueño.

XXV
(HISTORIA NATURAL DEL ESCOMBRO: AUSCHWITZ-BIRKENAU)

Cuando no quede ni una persona que recuerde, cuando no
reste en pie un solo tallo de nuestra memoria y nuestra voz
no valga su peso en sal, especias o ceniza, ¿cómo se verán
estos edificios? ¿Como los hallaron los pilotos aliados
con sus cámaras: lentas hileras de rectángulos abrazados a la
nieve? ¿costillas brotando en el aire hambriento?
¿O como los veo a través de Google Earth, barracas
relucientes como cráneos, rejas y alambres de púas limpios
y hasta corteses, todos más o menos somnolientos,
fingiendo la inocencia de los objetos abandonados
bajo la membrana reseca de mi pantalla? Vista desde el cielo,
la tierra es impermeable, lisa, bulímica. No tiene edad o acaso
tiene la edad de los mitos que se olvidan porque ya no sirven
a nadie. Alguien observará todo esto sin curiosidad o terror,
pupilas cubiertas por la resina de la distancia, como si el pasado
no pudiera ser el futuro y el tiempo apenas
fuera el país de lo ya visto. Cuando estemos masticando las
entrañas del suelo y no tengamos la tela de un nombre
para cubrir nuestra desnudez, no podremos advertirles
que la historia es un largo toque de queda donde
realmente nada concilia el sueño por completo.

XXVI

A todos nos daba miedo dormir bajo
el mismo techo que mi madre. En plena
madrugada, mientras descansábamos, sus
gritos nos despertaban súbitamente. Nunca he
escuchado a alguien chillar así, como una
desgarradura, una incandescencia, algo sacado
de un vientre animal. Sus cuerdas vocales
se gastaban cada noche; amanecía ronca, con
la voz porosa y agrietada. Gritaba como quien
abre un cráneo con sus propias manos, golpeándolo
contra una roca.

Pasaron algunos meses y a los
gritos en blanco se sumaron las risas, los gruñidos,
los pasos de baile. Ojos cerrados, gestos borrosos,
mi madre arrugaba el rostro, mostraba los dientes
con saña, sacudía el hocico o movía los brazos
tratando de ahuyentar un pájaro de esos que sólo
vuelan del otro lado de la vigilia. Cuando reía,
sus miembros se estiraban y contraían, tensos por
el esfuerzo. Sus carcajadas eran una ventana rota.
Permanecía en la cama

el resto de la noche, su
cuerpo se estrechaba hasta volverse una figura
diminuta, una formación geológica trabajada
por años de espera callada. Recordaba a esas
personas enterradas en Pompeya, tenía el mismo
deseo de hacerse piedra entre las piedras, la misma
anatomía mineral. Pegado a su pecho, un puño
cerrado: en su interior apretaba el nódulo que
había crecido en el seno izquierdo de mi abuela,
un corazón de utilería, un órgano de repuesto. Allí
guardaba la tos sucia, las visitas al hospital,

las pastillas, las noches en vela, todo sedimentado
ahora bajo la piel calcificada del sueño.

XXVII
(ANÁBASIS)

Un autobús en medio de la carretera. Así termina esto.
Un poco más atrás, abandonado, sin gasolina, hay un transporte
militar recorrido por agujeros de balas. El día en que nos
fuimos, guardamos toda la ropa que cupo en las mochilas y los
bolsos. Tomamos algunas joyas y las empacamos también; el
resto lo escondimos detrás de la nevera, pensando que
llegaría el día en que las necesitaríamos. Dinero oculto
en las medias, en la ropa interior. Mi hija pegó a la puerta
de la cocina una carta pidiendo a quienes vinieran
que no rompieran nada, por favor. Los retratos, las fotos
familiares, todo se lo van a llevar las hormigas, me dijo cuando
salimos del edificio, todo lo van a desmigajar poco a poco
para guardarlo en sus ciudades secretas. Mi hermano
tenía un contacto, alguien que nos podía conseguir un puesto
en alguno de los barcos, seguro, segurísimo, tan cierto
como el peso de un durazno o el olor a mañana del pan
sobre la mesa. Por un precio, claro. Pagamos. El autobús
en el que viajábamos fue detenido dos veces, una de ellas al
abandonar la ciudad, pero no nos bajaron. Adentro, nadie decía
nada: el horizonte nos pasaba su navaja por la lengua. Íbamos
pendientes del chillido intestino de los frenos, dejándonos
digerir por el calor, morosamente, sobre el forro de
plástico de los asientos. A veces recostaba la cabeza
contra el respaldar y trataba de imaginar cómo nos veríamos
desde lejos, moviéndonos en la carretera vacía, suturando
la distancia que nos separaba de la costa. No recuerdo quién
me había dicho que el océano no se parecía al agua,
que casi era un enorme papel arrugado por alguna manos
distraída. Pero esto lo pienso ahora. Cuando vimos
la costa, endeble, allá, sólo pensé: mar. Y decíamos: mar.
Que era como decir párpados inagotables. Que era como

decir hambre. Que era como decir la saliva del tiempo. Que era como decir el cabello interminable de los muertos. Que era como decir terror. El mar era el animal asustado más grande que habíamos visto. Marchábamos hacia él cuando escuchamos los disparos. Más adelante estaba el camión, soldados disparando a no sé quién, pequeños, aún remotos. El conductor aceleró. Quería atravesar a toda velocidad el fuego cruzado, no podíamos parar, no sabíamos qué harían con nosotros. Sin darnos la orden de alta, sin mediar un gesto, nos llenaron de balas. El conductor se detuvo de inmediato. Rato después, cuando se acabaron las detonaciones, vinieron por nosotros. Se llevaron a todas las mujeres, mataron a todos los hombres. Se fueron con prisa, ni siquiera nos registraron. Nos dejaron aquí tirados, la sal de la tierra. Así termina un autobús en medio de la carretera, en plena noche, triste como un perro en celo.

XXVIII

Palabras simples: lluvia, sol, casa, árbol, calle, madre, padre, hermano, risa, ahora, animal, miedo. Simples y confiables como dedos. Palabras complejas: nombre, número, golpe, grito, pregunta, bala, acusación, pasado, futuro, paciencia, animal, miedo. Cuando era niño, solía visitar a menudo el museo de ciencias naturales. Era un edificio grande, blanco, con un pórtico invadido por falsas columnas dóricas frente a una plaza circular. Al traspasar la entrada, a mano derecha, había un ala dedicada a las eras geológicas del planeta. Capas de tierra como párpados cerrados, telones de una obra que nadie sabe dónde empieza, países imposiblemente remotos, dormidos para siempre bajo nuestros pies. Lugares y períodos que no podía pronunciar con soltura, a los cuales sólo pusieron nombres para que no nos quemara las manos tanta lejanía. El planeta acaparaba vidas, mudaba de piel impunemente; quedaban los fósiles como pruebas, como instantáneas obscenas de un mundo que nada tiene que decirnos. Un poco más adelante, había toda un sección dedicada al reino animal. Encerrados tras vitrinas temblorosas, especímenes de toda clase miraban a la gente pasar con ojos de vidrio. Habían retirado meticulosamente las pieles de sus cuerpos muertos; las habían salado, rehidratado y curtido. Una vez secas y calladas, sin el rumor idiota de los fluidos vitales encerrado en ellas, habían sido colocadas sobre armazones rellenos. Aves de rapiña posadas sobre ramas de plástico y gomaespuma que crecieron fuera del tiempo, fieras de dientes amarillos y pelambre cariada, herbívoros distraídos, estancados en las más diversas poses, pastando, vigilando, cazando y siendo cazados, atrapados

en la mímica sorda del deseo. Yo caminaba con precaución,
la espalda contra la pared, tan aterrado como curioso,
repitiendo en voz baja todas las palabras simples que
podía recordar. Entre tanta fauna, esperaba toparme
en cualquier momento con un ángel disecado: mi abuela
me había dicho que eran las bestias de carga de dios.
Pero nunca alcanzaba el final de la sala. No había suficientes
palabras simples en el mundo, no para comprar mi paso
de una orilla a otra del miedo. Me retiraba con el mismo
cuidado, tratando de no atraer atención sobre mí, de no
perturbar ese sonambulismo frío. No he vuelto de adulto.
Esos animales amansados por los conservantes químicos me
dijeron lo que debían: el poema es un depredador
que ha sido cazado, desollado, macerado, cuya carne
se ha perdido y cuya piel cuelga, amenazante y ridícula,
sobre un esqueleto de palabras simples y palabras complejas.

XXIX

Ya que quieres escribir un poema de
amor, aquí hay unos pocos consejos.

No escribas demasiado. El amor, si breve,
dos veces amor. Nadie quiere ya confesiones
u obscenidades: las redes sociales y las
páginas porno han monopolizado el mercado
de la intimidad. Considera, pues, el haiku erótico.

La forma lo es todo. Pero no quieres un artilugio
complejo, una máquina anticuada. Los sonetos,
los romances, las coplas huelen un poco
como ese lomo de atún que tiene semanas
escondido en la nevera. Quieres un poema último
modelo, descapotable, de versos tuiteables, que
quepa por igual en las pajas del adolescente y
en el puño del maltratador doméstico.

(El espacio se inventó para que los poemas de amor
tengan donde ensayar su gimnasia presuntuosa).

Hay poemas de amor que están bastante gordos.
Comen con ansiedad, sin control alguno. Sus dedos,
nerviosos y grasientos, no dejan de manosear adjetivos
y símiles. Pesan sobre la página, sobre los párpados.
Los doctores advierten que, si no se ponen a dieta, si no
empiezan a hacer ejercicio, podrían desarrollar una
condición cardíaca o diabetes. Pero no hay nada más
triste que un poema de amor esdrújulo, voluminoso,
comiendo ensalada.

(Como ellos, a menudo el tiempo se ahoga

porque también quiere tragar demasiado).
No te ahorres labios de coral, dientes de perla, ojos de esmeralda: son accesorios vintage que no tardarán en ponerse de moda nuevamente. El rostro amado es un campo de juego (debes repetirte esto todas las mañanas al despertar), sus recovecos y pliegues se merecen las metáforas de abolengo más rancio, los piercings más deslumbrantes.

Si la desnudez del poema es insoportable, si no puedes con sus brazos flacos, sus piernas torcidas, su mirada bizca y demacrada, entonces vístelo con un epígrafe. Busca un proveedor que venda de marca y asegúrate de conseguir productos de talla adecuada. No compres donde Jaime Sabines o Joaquín Sabina –sobran los motivos.

Escoge bien tu clientela. Hay poemas de amor para estimular el apetito, poemas de amor para mejorar la circulación, poemas de amor para combatir el invierno, poemas de amor para quitar el sucio de los platos y las sartenes, poemas de amor que se venden como laxantes, poemas del amor después del amor, poemas de amor para borrar el acné, poemas de amor que curan la gripe, poemas de amor que borran (o fomentan, depende) el alcoholismo.

Trata de recordar un par de cosas. Tu poema de amor no deshará ninguna injusticia, no educará la sensibilidad de nadie, no dará de comer o beber a nadie, ni revertirá ninguna condena a muerte. Tu poema de amor no te conseguirá un céntimo de amor; apenas servirá para que algún hijo de puta convenza a su pareja de que no le volverá a pegar.

(Todos los poemas de amor son cómplices
de la violencia).

O, si acaso, valdrá para que
otros compren un polvo rápido alguna noche –nada
más. De todos modos, no te desanimes: el mercado de los
poemas de amor lleva décadas perdiendo terreno ante
el viagra y otros fármacos basados en el citrato
de sildenafilo. Nunca es tarde para cambiarse de ramo.

XXX
(A DAY IN THE LIFE)

Antes de que suene el despertador, el señor
ministro ya tiene los ojos abiertos: se levanta
con el sonido áspero de la herrería que esconde
bajo las costillas. Se cepilla los dientes, se
afeita. Sentado sobre la poceta, pantalones
alrededor de los tobillos, las manos unidas y la
frente inclinada en oración, pide a todos los
santos que intercedan por él, que lo libren
del cólico que pesa en sus intestinos, negro como
el pecado. Se ducha, viste y perfuma; un
café lo espera en la cocina. Toma el desayuno
con omeprazol, sentado muy derecho, la cabeza
sostenida gracias a la corbata; de no ser por
ese nudo, rodaría hasta quién sabe dónde. La
última vez fue una catástrofe: hallaron
la cabeza borracha y despeinada fuera de
un burdel –salió en todos los periódicos. Va a
la oficina con chofer y escolta, distraído
por las manchas que se hacen cada vez más
numerosas en sus manos. Primer rivotril del
día. El despacho lo recibe repleto de papeles,
tratados de comercio, tráfico bilateral,
compra y venta de bonos, acciones, propiedades,
glóbulos rojos, leucocitos, plaquetas, bilirrubina,
ceratonina, fíjate lo altos que están el azúcar
y el colesterol. Es urgente implementar el
control cambiario. La sangre siempre despilfarra.
Ibuprofeno para el dolor de cabeza, junto a las
actas del acuerdo de libre intercambio
trasatlántico y hematológico. Hay que cubrir
la tierra cruda con lo que se pueda, con lo que

tengamos a mano. Orden y progreso, o
lo más parecido. Segundo rivotril del día. Y
dios le impuso una tarea: da nombre a las bestias
que recorren el suelo, a las aves sin memoria ni
ambiciones, a los peces que nunca podrán
ganarse una sombra. El señor ministro obedeció.
Se dedicó a confeccionar nombres con voz
granulosa y, al poco rato, había llegado la hora
de los paquetes bancarios, las burbujas
inmobiliarias, la inflación con su dentadura
postiza y plomo en los ojos. Se había operado
el milagro eucarístico: la carne era estaño y el
vino petróleo. No era fácil, nada fácil. Tercer rivotril
del día: el milagro austero de la multiplicación de los
peces y el clonazepam, tal y como lo efectuó el hombre
de Galilea cuando inventó los intereses bancarios.
Y diclofenac para la espalda, por favor. Cuando
llega al bar, al whisky del fin de los tiempos,
está seguro de que su tensión ha subido, pero no
le queda losartan —una tragedia para la economía
nacional. Es imposible predecir qué sucederá con el
producto interno bruto si no se calma, pero la música
lo atormenta, no ha comido y el aluminio de la risa
ajena lo pone nervioso. Esta noche aterriza en la casa
de su amante, dispuesto a aprobar la explotación de
todos los recursos naturales que demande el desarrollo
de la nación. El destino del país cuelga de su temblor
cardiovascular, incandescente. Después de coger,
se encierra en el baño y orina tarareando *Imagine*. Ha
estado sonando en su cabeza durante todo el día.

XXXI
(HISTORIA NATURAL DEL ESCOMBRO: POMPEYA)

Afuera, lo de siempre: quioscos y tiendas, botellas de refresco
a ocho euros, gente espantando el bochorno con los
folletos turísticos. Autobuses con su ruido de metal exasperado
y el chillido largo de los frenos. Adentro sólo hay
piedra y calor, piedra concentrada en no quedarse dormida,
en no desmoronarse al ser mirada, piedra hecha de una
fe pastosa. Los restos de los edificios se estiran sobre el suelo
como la crónica de una larga fiebre, como si la pasión
solamente pudiera ser horizontal.

Pero este lugar no está vacío, sus
grietas y túneles están llenos de una vida minúscula, sin títulos ni
monumentos. Ciempiés, lombrices, grillos, escarabajos: toda una
ciudad sonámbula. Caminaba por ella, pisando las casas,
entrando sin ser invitado, intentando leer los grafitis y las
marcas dejadas en los muros, letras como frutos abiertos,
porosos. Observaba las letras y pensaba que el
ángel de la historia tiene alas de insecto desorientado,
mosca desquiciada por el olor lujoso de alguna cocina, una
cucaracha cuyas alas se inflan con un viento que proviene
de ninguna parte: va de aquí para allá, sacudido por la corriente,
mareado, hasta topar con una ventana: por ahí entra.

Años más tarde, en Québec,
encontré que alguien había escrito sox pistols en el cemento
fresco de una acera. La mañana era un coágulo de azul macizo; sobre
la frase había unas pocas hormigas atrapadas, incapaces de
levantar sus patas para librarse de la sustancia que se abrazaba
a ellas como una sordera. Haec est materia gloria nostræ, garabateó
Plinio por ahí, en las paredes del baño de la historia, junto a los números
de teléfono que prometen sexo fácil y un dibujo del césar masturbándose.

XXXII

(NANA PARA MALENA)

Duerme, hija, para que contigo duerman
todas las balas perdidas del mundo. Que
se aquieten por hoy los huesos desteñidos de
la tierra, que se detenga el cielo brusco
que cuelga sobre nosotros. El cuerpo te pide
esta paz a cambio de aguantar la voracidad
de tus manos, el peso en hambre de todas tus
preguntas –a cambio de tu estatura impaciente
bajo el sol. Duerme por quienes no pueden
descansar, contando las gotas de sudor frío
que la noche deja en las ventanas. Que el
terror pase a tu lado apenas como un
murmullo, como el cuerpo de una yegua adivinado
en la oscuridad. Que repose tu carne aturdida
por el sonido que producen los árboles al crecer.
Duerme en la otra orilla de estas palabras
con las que te arrullo, menos pesadas que tu
sombra, palabras que no te enseñé sino a medias
y que nada más sirven para hacerse invisible
poco a poco. Lejos de ti quienes siembran
dientes de rata en el suelo húmedo. Que
las patas de tu cama sean tan altas que no
la roce el mar; que los perros no vengan
a salmodiar junto a la puerta de tu cuarto.
Que el espacio te sea infiel, inagotable.
Y que todos los paraísos estén ya perdidos o
por perder. Puse en tu almohada raíces blancas,
hilos que bajan hasta el penúltimo aliento
de la infancia. Duerme tu cansancio liso: en
tu frente queda inmóvil la piedra blanda de tu risa.
Yo vendré a despertarte pronto, cuando el grano
de mañana que queda en tu piel se haya abierto.

XXXIII

Aquí tiene mi pasaporte. Sí, mi
visa está vigente. Tengo los papeles
que lo confirman. ¿Motivo del
viaje? Personal. No, no transporto
alcohol o tabaco. No, no llevo
conmigo alimentos sin pasteurizar,
materiales orgánicos, curiosidades
insalubres. No he estado recientemente
en una granja; no recuerdo la última vez
que estuve en una granja. No poseo licencia
para portar armas de fuego. Nunca he
tocado una. En mi bolso de mano
no hay botellas con más de 300 ml
de contenido. ¿Motivo del viaje?
Viajo por las mismas razones que
todo el mundo: por ingenuidad, por
creer lo que dicen los libros, que hay
un lugar donde no me alcanzará
mi nombre, donde podré tomarlo
finalmente en vano. No, en mi equipaje
no hay látigos, esposas, vibradores,
arneses. Tampoco documentos im
prescindibles para la paz de alguna
nación. No traslado especies animales
o vegetales; dejé las plantas carnívoras
en la infancia. Los órganos que llevo
están pulcramente guardados bajo mi piel,
algunos prematuramente cubiertos por
el óxido y la grasa. ¿Todas estas pastillas?
La circulación no puede quedarse estática,
no puede haber sangre perpleja en las
venas; la respiración no puede estancarse
en la tráquea como un puño de bruma:

me rompería los dientes y el paladar.
¿Motivo del viaje? Porque yo ya no soy
yo ni mi casa es ya mi casa. Usted, con
sus insignias y su uniforme, su himno
y su juramento a la bandera, no termina
de entender que un país es un puñado
de palabras robadas. Y algún día
hay que devolverlas. Eso hago justo
ahora: dejo las palabras por donde
puedo, donde me permiten, aunque ya
tengan un sabor rancio. Pago una
deuda con estas palabras legañosas, que
parpadean bajo la lámpara cenital. En la ciudad
donde nací, cada quien tiene sus deudas y
siempre hay alguien que las cobra. Allí, los
milagros son un peligro como cualquier otro,
una bala perdida, un desastre natural. Allí,
todas las pieles madrugan con la misma
resaca inocente ¿Motivo del viaje? Porque
en los lugares donde nadie habla mi lengua
el cuerpo es una desaparición: hay una
transparencia que gangrena de golpe la
carne, ninguna sílaba me carga, nadie
puede verme. Pero no viajo sin equipaje.
Mi ciudad está hecha de papel; se
dobla y se guarda en el bolsillo,
tiene la forma de un cuaderno, de un
tacto cómplice. En ella los santos atracan,
transmutan el agua en ron, manejan motos
empire y duermen su mínima eternidad
dentro de estatuas de arcilla. En mi
ciudad, llevamos nuestros muertos en el
bolsillo; no se los puede abandonar en
casa, desaparecen, se van al más allá o
los roban para venderlos –no dejan
a cambio ni un montoncito de sal.

No es realmente una ciudad: es una fiebre
lenta que se come el valle, trasnochada,
colérica. ¿Motivo del viaje? Desde hace
años sueño con una ballena que me traga,
me alberga durante meses detrás de sus dientes
de yeso, en la noche blanda de su estómago,
para finalmente escupirme en costas extrañas.

NOTAS

El poema VII está dedicado a la memoria de Eugenio Hernández.

El poema VIII está dedicado a Harry Abend.

El poema XI está dedicado a Juan Luis Landaeta.

El poema XII está dedicado a Víctor García Ramírez.

TRANSLATOR'S NOTE

When you translate, you are never alone. I mean this in a practical sense, not a romantic one. When you translate, you are always accompanied, writing-toward, speaking-with. You're an accomplice and an apprentice, too. You're writing a letter and answering it at the same time.

I translated *The Science of Departures*, by Adalber Salas Hernández, several years before a pandemic became "the" pandemic, before it upended our habits and our expectations and our speech. Rereading these poems now, though, I hear them a little differently. They're quieter somehow. Some sound desolate but also curious and often funny, a combination I find both sobering and strangely hopeful.

Each poem in this book explicitly plumbs some kind of loss, exile, illness, death, dispossession, political suppression, historical excavation, or chasm of language itself. They view our lives, our bodies, our stories and histories, as organic matter invariably eroded (or violently interrupted) over time. And they view our urge to understand these processes—to name them, study them, tell and retell them to ourselves and to each other—as necessarily insatiable. As something that keeps us alive not despite the fact but because we will never reach the clarity we long for.

Not all stories are poems, but all poems are stories. I'm grateful to Adalber—who is among my favorite storytellers, and as kind and generous a friend as they come—for telling me these, and for receiving what I've sent back in another language, another time.

—Robin Myers

ADALBER SALAS HERNÁNDEZ—poet, essayist, and translator—was born in Caracas, Venezuela. He is the author of seven collections of poetry, the most recent of which is *La ciencia de las despedidas* (Pre-Textos). He has published five collections of essays, as well as numerous translations from Portuguese, English, and French; these include works by Marguerite Duras, Antonin Artaud, Charles Wright, Mário de Andrade, Hart Crane, Pascal Quignard, Mark Strand, Lorna Goodison, Louise Glück, Yusef Komunyakaa, Anne Boyer, Frankétienne, and Patrick Chamoiseau. He has been a member of the editorial board for *Revista POESÍA* and *Buenos Aires Poetry*. He coordinates the collection Diablos Danzantes published by Amargord Ediciones and is pursuing a Ph.D. at New York University.

ROBIN MYERS is a poet and translator based in Mexico City. Recent translations include *Another Life* by Daniel Lipara (Eulalia Books), *Cars on Fire* by Mónica Ramón Ríos (Open Letter Books), *The Restless Dead* by Cristina Rivera Garza (Vanderbilt University Press), and *Animals at the End of the World* by Gloria Susana Esquivel (University of Texas Press). She was among the winners of the 2019 Poems in Translation Contest (Words Without Borders / Academy of American Poets). Selected translations have appeared in the *Kenyon Review*, *The Baffler*, *The Common*, *Harvard Review*, *Two Lines*, *Waxwing*, *Asymptote*, *Los Angeles Review of Books*, and elsewhere. She writes a monthly column for *Palette Poetry*.

Juana I, by Ana Arzoumanian, translated by Gabriel Amor

Waveform, by Amber DiPietra and Denise Leto

Style, by Dolores Dorantes, translated by Jen Hofer

PQRS, by Patrick Durgin

The Pine-Woods Notebook, by Craig Dworkin

Propagation, by Laura Elrick

Tarnac, a preparatory act, by Jean-Marie Gleize, translated by Joshua Clover with Abigail Lang and Bonnie Roy

Hieroglyphs of the Inverted World, by Rob Halpern

The Chilean Flag, by Elvira Hernández, translated by Alec Schumacher

título / title, by Legna Rodríguez Iglesias, translated by Katherine M. Hedeen

Stage Fright: Selected Plays from San Francisco Poets Theater, by Kevin Killian

The Kenning Anthology of Poets Theater: 1945-1985, edited by Kevin Killian and David Brazil

The Grand Complication, by Devin King

There Three, by Devin King

Insomnia and the Aunt, by Tan Lin

Dream of Europe: selected seminars and interviews: 1984-1992, by Audre Lorde, edited by Mayra Rodríguez Castro

The Compleat Purge, by Trisha Low

Ambient Parking Lot, by Pamela Lu

Some Math, by Bill Luoma

Festivals of Patience: The Verse Poems of Arthur Rimbaud, translated by Brian Kim Stefans

The Dirty Text, by Soleida Ríos, translated by Barbara Jamison and Olivia Lott

Several Rotations, by Jesse Seldess

Left Having, by Jesse Seldess

Who Opens, by Jesse Seldess

Grenade in Mouth: Some Poems of Miyó Vestrini, translated by Anne Boyer and Cassandra Gillig and edited by Faride Mereb

French Unpublished Poems & Facsimilie 1958-1960, by Miyó Vestrini, translated by Patrick Durgin, edited, designed and printed by Faride Mereb

Hannah Weiner's Open House, by Hannah Weiner, edited by Patrick Durgin

Coronavirus Haiku, by Worker Writers School, edited by Mark Nowak

KENNINGEDITIONS.COM